THE
POWER
AND THE
GLORY

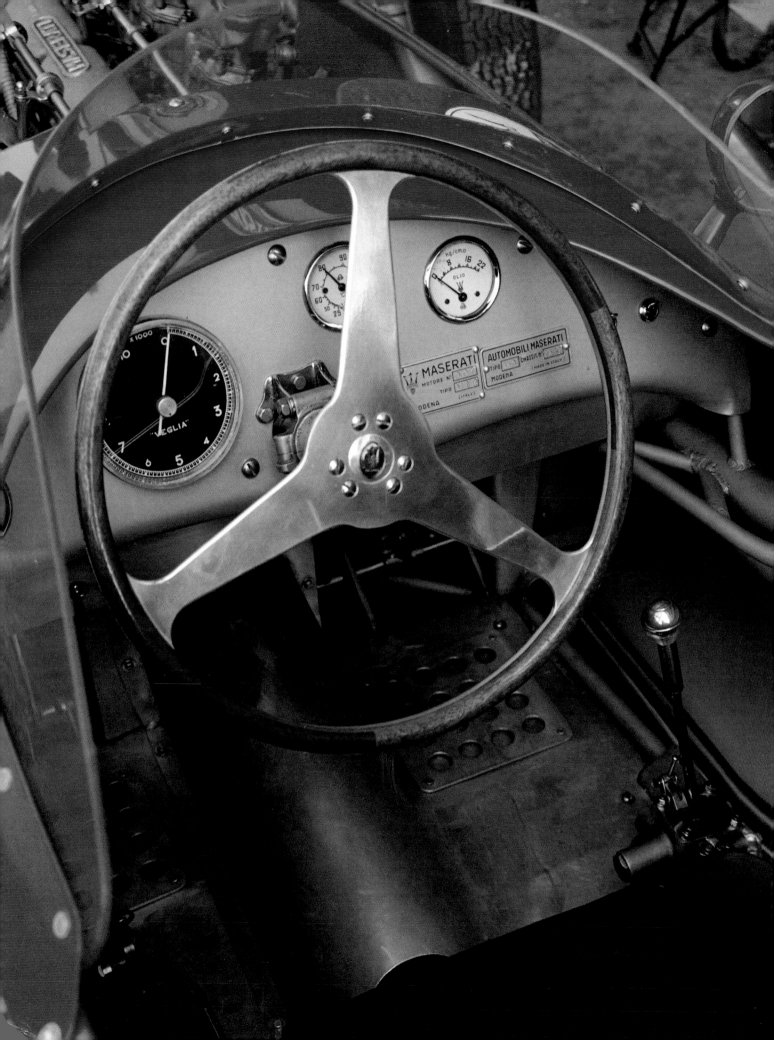

THE POWER AND THE GLORY

A CENTURY OF MOTOR RACING

IVAN RENDALL

BBC BOOKS

© Ivan Rendall and John Gau Productions 1991
The right of Ivan Rendall to be identified as the Author of this work has been
asserted in accordance with the Copyright, Designs and Patents Act 1988.

ISBN 0 563 36468 8

Designed by Linda Blakemore
Picture research by Sarah Matthews

Published by BBC Books
a division of BBC Enterprises Limited
Woodlands, 80 Wood Lane, London W12 0TT

First published 1991
Reprinted 1991 (twice)
First paperback edition published 1992

Set in 11/14pt Sabon by Butler & Tanner Limited, Frome
Printed and bound in Great Britain by Butler & Tanner Limited, Frome
Colour separations by Technik Limited, Berkhamsted
Jacket printed by Belmont Press, Northampton

ENDPAPERS Ferrari 500 engine.
FRONTISPIECE Cockpit of the Maserati 250.
OPPOSITE Mrs Gwenda Stewart setting up a new world 10-mile record
driving a supercharged 2-litre straight-eight Derby-Miller at Montlhéry, 1930.
Painting by F. Gordon Crosby.
PAGES 6–7 Barney Oldfield in a Blitzen Benz at Indianapolis, 1910.
Painting by Peter Helck.
PAGE 9 Ayrton Senna, San Marino Grand Prix, 1991.

PICTURE CREDITS

CONTENTS

Barney Oldfield

ELCK

INTRODUCTION

The urge to compete and the will to win are powerful human instincts. They are the driving forces behind many human endeavours and they govern a great many aspects of our lives. But competition between teams or individuals is the very essence of one human activity – sport. Many types of sport were developed largely as a way of channelling human competitiveness in a harmless, even productive, way.

Motor racing is no exception. Speed was the measure of the motor car: within a few years of its invention, car manufacturers wanted to see who could build the fastest car and drivers wanted to find out who could drive them faster than anybody else. An exciting new sport, geared to the priorities of a technological age and the themes of the twentieth century, had been born.

Like any sport, participation in motor racing is pyramid-shaped. The broad base is made up of thousands of drivers all over the world who compete every week in hundreds of events organized for all manner of different types of car. They race against each other in order to progress up the pyramid. Some never move

from the bottom, some struggle a little way up, enjoy the competition and the lifestyle, but lack the ability to go any further and stay there. A few go right to the top where, at any one time, only several dozen drivers worldwide compete for the major prizes and for most of the glory.

Ever since the beginning of the sport that elite has produced some of the popular heroes of their day. Driving the fastest and most powerful cars in the world to (and sometimes beyond) their limits has made them artists in the modern age. The rare combination of natural talents and acquired skills, needed to make them masters of their often dangerous profession, has expressed something about the pace and vitality of our century.

The Power and the Glory is about the cars and the drivers who have reached the top of the pyramid. It traces the development of the sport at that level over nearly a hundred years. It is a general history of motor racing and as such it is necessarily selective; it cannot hope to be either a complete or even a comprehensive record of the sport.

CHAPTER ONE

A CENTURY OF MOTOR RACING

On Sunday 30 May 1982 the Indianapolis Motor Speedway was packed to capacity for the jewel in the crown of American motor racing, the biggest single-day sporting event in the world: the 'Indy' 500. It was a day rich in the enduring images and abiding attractions of motor racing – fast, beautiful motor cars, pushed to their limits by gifted drivers who were breaking records in the pursuit of victory and a share of the purse of over $2m.

Two men had dominated the race, and with 10 of the 200 laps to go, the crowd began to sense an exciting finish. Both drivers were previous winners. Gordon Johncock, a veteran of 46 in his 18th Indy, was in the lead. Rick Mears, a comparative youngster of 31, was 10 seconds behind.

Two laps later Mears had cut the lead to 8 seconds; another two and it was down to 6 seconds. It was to be a duel to the finish; Mears could win and the crowd knew it. As the cars began the penultimate lap there was half a second between them.

It was a compelling moment. Four hundred thousand people at the track, and millions watching on television, followed them round the $2\frac{1}{2}$-mile rectangular circuit. On the final bend of the final lap, Mears made his challenge. He positioned himself to overtake but Johncock moved to the centre of the track, holding him off just long enough to cross the line .16 of a second in front – the narrowest victory in Indy's history.

The crowd roared with pleasure at the split-second result; 'Gordy' basked in the glory of the Winner's Circle with the trophy. His average speed (162.069 mph) was a new race record.

LEFT **Speed: Gordon Johncock at Indianapolis.**

Speed – a craving for the sight, sound and smell of it – was the initial attraction of motor racing and has remained so for both drivers and spectators since the first decade of the sport. The first organized race was in 1895 on the open roads of France, from Paris to Bordeaux and back. The winner, Emile Levassor, drove a 4-bhp Panhard-Levassor which had a top speed of 18.5 mph. Such events were both a proving ground and a shop window for the infant automobile industry. Winning was all important and the speed of racing cars increased dramatically in those early years at a rate which has never been matched. Fernand Charron won a similar type of race from Paris to Lyons in 1900 in a Panhard with an average speed of 38.6 mph and a top one of around 50 mph. A car which could do 50 mph was a huge attraction for the thousands of people who were out on the 353-mile route.

In those heady, heroic, days the key to higher speed was greater engine size. Most engines were around 12–13 litres, but one of the biggest, in a Christie in the Grand Prix of 1907, was nearly 20 litres. Massive engines were mounted in long, often flimsy, chassis, with only primitive brakes. These monsters weighed around a ton, and it took not only physical strength but courage to drive them at speed. By 1908, 100 mph was common down the straights on rough, dusty roads.

Various attempts had been made to curb the trend towards ever-bigger engines by imposing restrictions on weight, piston area, fuel consumption and engine size. Race organizers laid down a specification, or formula, determining which cars could take part. In 1908, the Grand Prix Formula was a maximum piston area of 117 sq.in. and a minimum weight limit of 1150 kg. By 1914, limiting engine size was seen as the best way to regulate racing and a 4.5-litre 'formula' was introduced. In most types of racing, cars have been built to a formula, usually based on engine size, ever since. As technology advances, the governing bodies change the formula and engine designers are

LEFT Size: a 1903 Napier, Britain's leading contender in the age of the monster racing car. Many British drivers preferred the superior French cars of the period, such as Panhard.

encouraged to improve the performance of their creations by new technical improvements.

Over the years, speeds have risen steadily. By the late 1930s, a remarkable series of Mercedes cars was capable of 200 mph down the straights. Hermann Lang won in one at the Avus circuit near Berlin in 1937 at an average speed of 162.61 mph, with his rival Ernst von Delius just 1.6 seconds behind at the finish – an interesting comparison with Gordon Johncock and Rick Mears at Indianapolis 45 years later. The fastest cars built for circuit racing were the Porsche 917 sports cars. In 1971, one driven by Gérard Larrousse and Vic Elford in the Le Mans 24-hour race was timed along the famous Mulsanne straight at 240.1 mph.

The ethos of speed which permeates motor racing is so powerful that it sometimes obscures the fact that speed alone is not the only objective of a racing driver. In the sense of turning in the fastest laps consistently, speed comes because the driver is doing rather more than simply driving flat out wherever he can. The fastest men are those for whom the car, and its relationship with the track, becomes an extension of their mental awareness and physical senses. The smooth and accurate driver who can balance his car carefully on the right line, at the right speed for every part of the track, will always beat the man who is rough with the car and drives erratically. As in any field of human endeavour, there are those who take naturally to driving fast and those who have to work hard at it.

Races are won by drivers, not cars, and when they win in an inferior machine their victories go down in history. The Monaco Grand Prix in 1961 was just such an event. Formula One cars had just been reduced from 2.5 to 1.5 litres and Ferrari had a brand-new model, the Type 156 'Sharknose', with a new and powerful V6 engine. They also had a works team of three top drivers: Richie Ginther, Phil Hill, who became World Champion that year, and Wolfgang von Trips. Stirling Moss was driving a Lotus 18, the previous year's car which, even though it had been re-engined, was less powerful by 20 per cent. It was entered by Rob Walker's private racing team.

THE BIRTH OF A TWENTIETH-CENTURY HERO

The first racing drivers were usually wealthy, often titled men for whom racing was a sporting diversion. That tradition, of the gifted, gentleman amateur, continued into the 1950s before giving way to the highly professional blend of sportsmen and businessmen who dominate all branches of the sport today. Most of the current top drivers started out in amateur races, displaying their talents in karts, rallying or saloon-car racing before graduating to the big league.

Whatever route they take, they have always been the stuff of modern popular heroes. Young men with glamorous lifestyles, masters of powerful machines, they willingly face danger in events which put a high premium on individual achievement. In an age of mass communications, this potent mixture has been magnified around the world by magazines, radio, newsreels and television. A handful of drivers at the top have been transformed from sportsmen into international superstars.

ABOVE **The professional: Alain Prost, French (b. 1955). World Champion in 1985, 1986 and 1989, Prost epitomized the racing driver of the 1980s. Wealthy through winning and sponsorship, he also brought charm and humour to the track and always** thrilled the crowd by driving to win, especially in battles with the Brazilian driver, Ayrton Senna.

BELOW **The racing driver as superman: the young Brazilian, Mauricio Gugelmin (b. 1963).**

ABOVE LEFT **The amateur: Charles Jarrott, British (1877–1944).** Jarrott was a successful driver, but his lasting contribution to the sport was as its early chronicler. In 1906, he wrote *Ten Years of Motors and Motor Racing*, a classic account of racing on open roads which was also a lament that his sport was being tainted by commercialism.

LEFT **The racing driver as sportsman.**

ABOVE LEFT The moment of victory: the Italian driver Tazio Nuvolari crosses the finishing line to win the 1935 German Grand Prix. His Alfa Romeo P.3 was out of date and under-powered, but by sheer driving skill he beat the German drivers in their more powerful Mercedes and Auto Unions on their own ground, at the Nürburgring.

ABOVE RIGHT Savouring victory: it was Nuvolari's greatest race and arguably the greatest victory in the history of the sport.

BELOW The joy of victory: Jim Clark and Colin Chapman celebrate with a lap of honour at Brands Hatch in 1963. Clark had clinched the World Championship for the first time at Monza the previous week, in the revolutionary monocoque Lotus 25. The car had won the World Constructors' Championship for Chapman.

Ginther took the lead at the start but on lap 12 Moss overtook him, driving the race of his life in the underpowered Lotus, always trying for the perfect lap, analysing every tiny mistake, too near the kerb here, too far away there. Moss was under pressure from the Ferraris for the rest of the 100-lap race; the gap between them was rarely more than 5 seconds and he won by 3.6 seconds.

Moss's win at Monaco and Tazio Nuvolari's triumph in the German Grand Prix in 1935 when he too was in an obsolete car are two of the greatest victories in motor racing. That winning touch comes from deep inside a driver: concentration, discipline, fitness, confidence, courage even; but above all, the will to win by however narrow a margin.

Denis Hulme, World Champion in 1967, explained the difference between winning and losing: 'You've tried everything you know for 3 hours; you've used every bit of skill you've got and it's not done you much good. No one knows how much you've tried except you. To tell anyone wouldn't get you anywhere ... the name of the game is to win; if you don't it's not much fun. The difference between winning and losing is immense.'

RIGHT The rewards of victory: a glittering place in motor racing's most famous hall of fame – the Borg Warner trophy with its silver busts of all the Indianapolis 500 winners. The total purse for the Indianapolis 500 in 1990 was $5,723,725.

ABOVE Louis Renault and his riding mechanic, François Szisz, during the ill-fated 1903 Paris-Madrid race in which Louis' brother Marcel was killed. Louis gave up racing after the tragedy, but Szisz went on to drive for Renault. In 1906, he won the first-ever Grand Prix at Le Mans.

LEFT Rick Mears' pit crew at the 1988 Indianapolis 500, the year he won his third Indy and set a new lap record of 220.453 mph.

The first motor races took place on the public highways, but the roads of Europe had been made for horses, carts and carriages, not cars driven by men intent on overtaking each other at 70 mph. The driver in front could see clearly, but those behind drove in a dust storm. Competitive driving – on public roads, in ever-faster cars, in poor visibility – had become too dangerous even for a sport. It took a disaster to stop it.

Early in the morning of 24 May 1903, the cream of European racing drivers set off on the most ambitious inter-town race yet, from Paris to Madrid. Reports of carnage *en route* were soon coming back: dozens of accidents, some of them fatal. One of the fatalities was Marcel Renault, a founder of the great French car firm. Just south of Poitiers, 125 miles from Bordeaux, approaching the village of Couhe-Verac behind Léon Théry, he was driving in the dust when Théry went into a sharp left-hand bend. Renault did not see it coming, went off the road, overturned, and was fatally injured; his mechanic survived. The French Government stopped the event at Bordeaux. It was the last inter-town race: two drivers, two mechanics, and four spectators had been killed. The rugged, carefree, pioneering era of motor racing was over.

A classic racing car: the 1908, 12-litre Itala in which Alessandro
Cagno and his mechanic, Cecil Bianchi, came 11th in the 1908
Grand Prix at Dieppe; it was also raced, and won, at Brooklands.
In its day, this venerable machine could do over 100 mph.

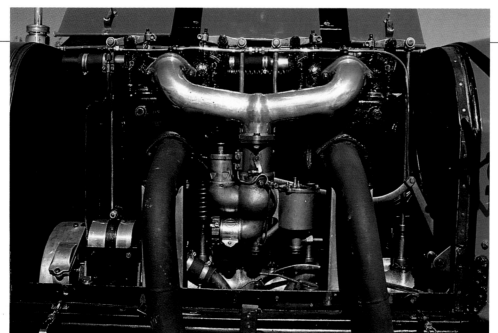

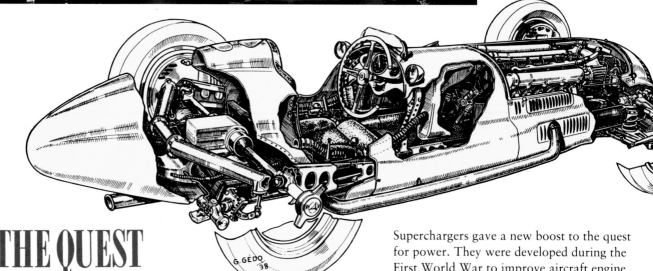

THE QUEST FOR POWER

The heart and lungs of a racing car is the engine and getting more horsepower per litre of engine capacity has absorbed designers throughout the history of motor racing.

Early racing engines were big and slow revving. The 12-litre 1908 Itala produced 10 bhp/litre. Technical improvements, especially the double overhead camshaft which was introduced in 1911, helped to bring about a reduction in the size of engines while increasing their power output per litre. The 4.5-litre Mercedes which won the 1914 Grand Prix produced 115 bhp at 3200 rpm, or 25.5 bhp/litre.

Superchargers gave a new boost to the quest for power. They were developed during the First World War to improve aircraft engine performance in the thinner air at high altitudes by forcing the fuel/air mixture into the cylinder using a mechanically driven compressor. The supercharged Mercedes cars of the late 1930s produced over 100 bhp/litre.

Turbochargers, where the compressor is driven by a small turbine in the exhaust, thus eliminating mechanical losses, dramatically increased power output from 1977. By 1981, turbocharged Renault engines were producing 520 bhp from 1.5-litre engines or 346.6 bhp/litre. By 1986, BMW was getting 1300 bhp from 1.5 litres or 866 bhp/litre.

With power output spiralling upwards, the authorities insisted that cars be fitted with 'pop-off' valves which limited the pressure turbochargers could generate. In 1989, turbochargers were banned altogether.

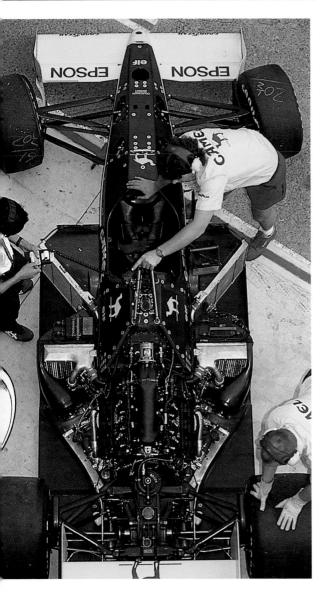

As one form of road racing came to an abrupt end, so another was emerging to take its place. In 1902, the Belgian Motor Club had arranged a race on roads closed for the purpose in the Ardennes. Competitors had to drive six times round a 53.5-mile circuit. The event was a great success, attracting a huge crowd of spectators and 75 drivers. Conditions were much the same as for the inter-town races except that competitors generally had the road to themselves. It was full of incident: Camille Jenatzy crashed shortly after the start; Pierre de Crawhez, the organizer, hit Evance Coppice's car; Léon Théry hit a cow; Pierre de Caters, blinded by Charles Jarrot's dust cloud, drove into a wall. Drivers drank reviving draughts of champagne from the bottle. The crowd was gripped by the battle for first place between Jarrot for Panhard and Fernand Gabriel for Mors. Jarrot won, having narrowly missed slamming into Gabriel who had stopped to replace a broken chain.

Such events became the norm on the Continent and motor racing began to change from an adventure into an organized sport. Prize money attracted a new breed of professional drivers as well as sportsmen and grandstands were built for spectators. Racing became a social occasion: the Kaiserpreis, held in the Taunus forest near Frankfurt in 1907 to mark Germany's international debut, was attended by the Emperor Wilhelm II with all the trappings of a state occasion.

Road racing in this form survived for over half a century giving rise to names resonant in the history of the sport: Targa Florio, Vanderbilt Cup, Le Mans, Carrera Panamericana, Reims, Tourist Trophy, Dundrod and – the greatest of them all – the Mille Miglia.

By the 1950s, these races were becoming a dangerous anachronism, even on closed roads. It took a series of disasters to bring change.

The first was at Le Mans in 1955. By this time its circuit of closed roads was well protected by barriers, but a Mercedes driven by Pierre Levegh touched another car and somersaulted into the crowd, killing over 80 spectators. The accident was seen as evidence of the inherent danger of motor racing. Events were cancelled all over Europe.

ABOVE Racing cars are essentially functional, with speed as their goal. But they have always also been objects of great beauty. Amongst the most pleasing are those which came from the pen of Ettore Bugatti, an Italian living in France. His '*pièce de résistance*' was the Bugatti Type 35. Its most distinctive feature is the radiator: based on a horse shoe, it reflects Bugatti's great love of horses; the badge is a perfect elipse.

RIGHT Bugatti's aesthetic sense was inherited by his son, Jean, who designed the coachwork for the great Bugattis of the 1930s. The body panels were moulded to take two colours; yellow and black was a recurring combination for the roadster cars.

That year's Mille Miglia, a 1000-mile race through northern Italy, had already been run. Thousands of spectators had gathered along the route and drivers had been faced with crowds which spilled on to the road, a path magically opening up as the cars hurtled down the straights.

Against that background, the Mille Miglia was held again in 1956, despite protests, and again in 1957. Alfonso de Portago, lying fourth in a Ferrari, burst a tyre at over 160 mph, flattened a telegraph

Léon Théry on his way to winning the 1905 Gordon Bennett Trophy race for France in a Richard-Brasier; behind is Charles Rolls in a Wolseley Beetle. Having drawn No. 1 Théry started first, an advantage as he was not in anybody else's dust.

ABOVE Count Giulio Masetti driving a Mercedes to victory on the dusty roads which were still a feature of the famous Targa Florio road race in Sicily in 1922. He was killed in the same event in 1926 when his car overturned.

ABOVE RIGHT Louis Chiron driving a Talbot to win on the road circuit at Reims in the Grand Prix de France in 1949.

pole, then ploughed into a group of spectators killing nine people, five of them children. It was the last Mille Miglia and most other road races followed it into history soon afterwards. The Targa Florio, run in the mountains of Sicily, managed to hang on until 1973.

Road racing had finally been tamed. The tradition of closing off public roads continues today at prestige events of long standing such as the Le Mans 24-hour race and Monaco Grand Prix, but the circuits are temporarily brought up to the safety standards which prevail at specially built tracks.

Specially built circuits started in Britain long before the First World War; road racing in the Continental manner had always been banned there, or rather, banished to the fringes such as Ireland. From the 1890s, British drivers had to go to other European countries to race and British spectators and manufacturers suffered as a consequence. To counter this, in 1906 a wealthy Surrey landowner, Hugh F. Locke-King, called together enthusiasts to plan a race track on which the British industry

could also test and display its cars. Brooklands was opened in 1907 and its name became synonymous with racing in Britain. It had banking at the corners and spectators could see large parts of the 2.75-mile, roughly oval circuit from the various enclosures. The tradition of racing on specially built tracks had been born.

America followed suit in 1908 with the Indianapolis Motor Speedway. On the Continent, tracks combining banked sections with stretches of road were built after the First World War, giving rise to another series of evocative names: Monza in Italy, Montlhéry in France, and Avus in Germany. Much shorter than the circuits used for traditional

road races, and extremely fast, they were ideal for spectators. But their important feature was their permanence, enabling organizers to charge an entry fee, an economic necessity from the 1920s onwards.

Circuits which simulated road-racing conditions – such as the Nürburgring in Germany which was opened in 1927 and Donington in Britain which was widened to take cars in 1933 – were specially built in Europe. This combination of two traditions – a specially built track with a variety of bends and straights, with grandstands and permanent facilities for drivers and spectators – became the model in Europe. Most Formula One races today are held on this kind of circuit.

LEFT Avus banking: Luigi Fagioli at speed on the North Curve in a streamlined Auto Union, May 1937. The Berlin circuit was first used in 1922 but the steep banking was not added until 1936, apparently at the suggestion of Adolf Hitler. The addition made it the fastest track at the time.

BELOW Brooklands: the first purpose-built motor-racing circuit in the world. It was opened in 1907 for racing, but was also a venue for record attempts. The first was by Selwyn Edge in a Napier, who set out to break the record for distance travelled in 24 hours. Over 28/29 June 1907, he covered 1581.75 miles at an average speed of 65.905 mph, a record which stood for 18 years.

Racing cars of whatever period represent the high technology of their times and they need constant, skilled attention to remain at peak performance. In the pioneering years of long-distance road racing there were few facilities *en route* and it was essential to carry a mechanic in the car. His task ranged from quite major jobs, such as changing a valve, to topping up water, fuel and oil, or slashing off worn tyres with a knife and forcing on new tubes and outer casings. While racing, he watched the engine instruments and warned the driver when other cars were approaching.

It was an uncomfortable and thankless task – sharing all the dangers for little of the glory – but it was exciting and there were plenty of volunteers. Some riding mechanics used their precarious job, with its intimate view of driving technique, as an apprenticeship and a way to become racing drivers themselves.

As engines became more reliable and races were run over shorter distances, risking two people in the car began to look increasingly like habit rather than necessity. The Automobile Association of America opened the way for the first single-seat

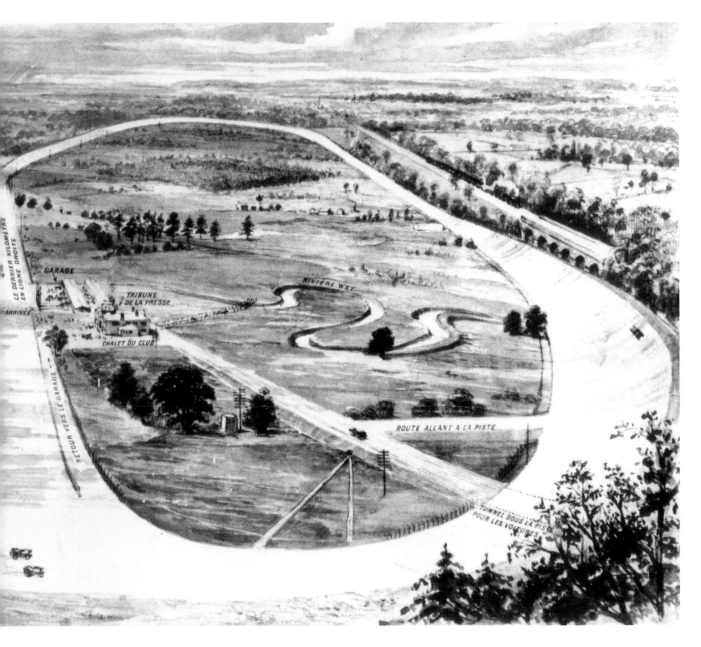

cars in 1923 by dispensing with riding mechanics. In Europe, however, they continued to occupy the second seat despite mounting pressure from some drivers and manufacturers that they be dropped. Eventually, disaster sealed their fate. In the 1924 Spanish Grand Prix at San Sebastian, conditions were wet and the British driver Kenelm Lee Guinness, driving a Sunbeam, crashed. He was injured, but his mechanic Jack Barrott was killed. The following year, riding mechanics were banned in Grands Prix.

Mechanics were confined to the pits where their job was no less demanding in terms of accuracy and speed, and the link between the driver and his first line of support remained as strong as ever. If they fumbled a driver might die; seconds wasted in the pits could mean the difference between winning and losing. Today at Indianapolis, for example, a good pit stop – putting in 40 gallons of fuel and changing all four wheels – is between 11 and 12 seconds. Inevitably, mistakes do happen. In 1981, when Rick Mears came in for a pit stop during the Indy 500 the hose which delivers fuel under pressure was not connected properly. He and some of the pit crew were soaked in fuel which caught fire. Mears leapt out of the car and his father put out the flames with an extinguisher, but driver and crew finished up in hospital, Mears with face burns for which he needed skin grafts.

Winning races is about saving split seconds on the track and in the pits, but it is the ingenuity of designers and their pursuit of engineering excellence which ultimately gives drivers a competitive edge. Teams that are serious about winning have to go to what seem extraordinary lengths to improve their cars. An example is Jaguar, who won the Le Mans 24-hour race in 1988 after years of work. Richard West, the company's spokesman, used the car's gearbox to illustrate the point: 'Many people would probably consider us crazy to try to find an engineering solution to trim say hundredths of a second off a gear change, but at somewhere like Le Mans, where there are literally thousands of gear changes during the course of the 24-hour race, it doesn't take a genius to work out the sort of saving that can be made.'

ABOVE **Motoring men:** Henry Ford (far left) with the four founders of the Indianapolis Motor Speedway (left to right) Arthur C. Newby, Frank H. Wheeler, Carl G. Fisher and James A. Allison.

RIGHT **The line-up:** the first 500-mile event took place on 30 May 1911. It has been held every year since then except when the United States has been at war.

ABOVE RIGHT **The winner:** Ray Harroun in his Marmon 'Wasp' wins the first '500' after 6 hours 42 minutes on the bricks at an average speed of 74.59 mph. He was the only car in the race without a riding mechanic and the first driver to use a rear-view mirror.

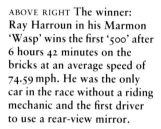

RIGHT **The spectacle:** the Indianapolis 500 is run in late May each year, on the Sunday of Memorial Day Weekend. It is the culmination of a month-long festival of motor racing during which 750,000 people go through the turnstiles.

FAR RIGHT **The poster:** Indianapolis has never been shy of its place in motor racing history. In over 80 years it has become part of America's heritage. In 1987, it was declared a National Historic Landmark.

THE 'BRICKYARD'

The young American automobile industry, like its British counterpart, felt the need for a track on which to test and promote its products. In August 1909, it got one: the Indianapolis Motor Speedway, today, with Le Mans, one of the longest serving and most famous venues for the sport. The original crushed stone and asphalt surface disintegrated under racing conditions and, in December that year, 3.2 million paving bricks were laid giving the track its colloquial name.

One of the disadvantages of tracks like Brooklands and Indianapolis, 'speedbowls' as they became known, was that they did not simulate road conditions and cars were built specially for them, stunting development. The US automobile industry virtually pulled out of racing between the wars, leaving racing to the specialists.

In 1945, the track was in disrepair and it seemed that its days were numbered. But it was taken over by Tony Hulman and turned into the multi-million dollar business it is today.

As engineers and drivers measure victory in ever-smaller fractions of a second, so others have to measure such progress in terms of hard cash. The economics of motor racing at its top level have always been based on the principle that winning costs money – but that the only thing worth investing in is winning.

Writing in 1906, when the sport was only 10 years old, Charles Jarrot lamented that the firms with the most money would always win because they could give their drivers an advantage over pure sportsmen like himself: 'The result is that only men who make it their business to drive these cars can hope to be successful ... the curse of commercialism is the ruin of every sport.'

Jarrot had reluctantly recognized that motor racing was a business, but he also predicted that public interest would decline as a result of reducing it to that level. In that he could not have been more wrong. In the end it was the steady growth in public interest, and people's willingness to pay to watch races, that kept the financial lifeblood flowing. Working on the principle that once you have a crowd you might as well sell them something, advertising space at race tracks became an additional source of income.

ABOVE Early commercialism: '*Sept Chemins*' on the Lyons circuit during the 1924 French Grand Prix. This corner was a popular place for the promotion of tyres, lamps and fuel. The 1924 race was the first French Grand Prix with prize money: 100,000 francs (and a huge Lyons sausage).

OPPOSITE AND BELOW Twin financial pillars of the modern sport: alcohol and tobacco.

A CENTURY OF PROGRESS: MERCEDES-BENZ

Mercedes-Benz is a combination of the two oldest car manufacturers in the world. Gottlieb Daimler was an engine builder who experimented first with a motorized cycle in 1885 and later with a boat and a carriage. Daimler cars became known as Mercedes after a wealthy Austrian businessman Emil Jellinek, who lived in Nice, became a distributor for Daimler cars in France at the turn of the century. He insisted, as part of the deal, that the cars be marketed as Mercedes, the name of his daughter. Daimler agreed, the name caught on and was soon adopted for all Daimler cars. The three-pointed star symbol was adopted in 1911, signifying the companies three areas of operation: land, sea and air.

Karl Benz had taken out the first patent for a motor car in 1886. Both companies built high-quality cars and engines and they both used racing as a means of promoting their products. In 1926 the two companies merged, to form Mercedes-Benz, adopting Daimler's three-pointed star with the Benz laurel wreath as their common symbol.

Mercedes has been very successful in using racing to promote its cars, in particular Grand Prix racing before the First World War and in the 1930s, Grand Prix and sports-car racing in the 1950s, and sports-car racing in the 1980s.

ABOVE In 1955 Mercedes won the World Sports Car Championship with its 300 SLR sports racing car. The team had three of the best drivers of their day: Juan Manuel Fangio (1), Stirling Moss (2) and Karl Kling (3) who came first, second and fourth in Germany's Eifelrennen that year.

LEFT The company pulled out of racing the same year, not returning until the late 1980s with the Sauber-Mercedes prototype sports cars. Peter Sauber tempted Mercedes back after successfully using its V8 turbocharged engine in his own cars. They won all but one of the races in the World Sports Car Championship in 1989 to take the title, with Jean-Louis Schlesser winning the Drivers' title as well.

FAR LEFT History and racing combined to promote the Mercedes-Benz name in the 1930s: an 1893 Benz Victoria and 1934 Mercedes W25.

In the 1930s, the link between money and winning was most vividly shown when the Nazi Party realized that a successful national motor-racing industry would be a powerful symbol of technical prowess. The Transport Ministry invested directly in Daimler-Benz and Auto Union, with cash bonuses for finishing first, second or third. In five years, from virtually a standing start, these cars completely dominated the sport at Grand Prix level.

In the late 1950s, racing went through a technical revolution which laid the foundations of a new economic order for the sport. It started in Britain with Charles Cooper, a Surrey garage-owner who started building racing cars after the Second World War. He built a mid-engined car to challenge the big names of Maserati, Mercedes and Ferrari. The Australian driver Jack Brabham won the World Constructors' Championship for Cooper and the World Drivers' Championship title for himself in 1959, repeating the double in 1960. In a very short time, all cars in Grands Prix had their engines in the rear. Colin Chapman of Lotus improved on the Cooper design and, in 1963, Jim Clark managed the double for Britain again. Two years later, the Clark and Chapman partnership took on America's finest at Indianapolis and beat the front-engined cars on their home ground.

The technical revolution was complete, but the revolutionaries, led by Chapman, went on to change the economic structure and organization of the sport. Advertising on racing cars had been banned in Europe; it was frowned upon by the governing bodies. However, the new breed of 'kit car' manufacturers, always looking for money to improve their products, saw it as a rich new source of finance. Chapman was the first to do a deal, with John Player cigarettes. He painted his cars in the colours of their Gold Leaf brand and entered his team as Gold Leaf Team Lotus.

National racing colours, which dated back to 1900, were soon replaced by the liveries of cigarette manufacturers, cosmetics firms and breweries who gradually became the paymasters of the sport. Winners were what the sponsor wanted and, with

ABOVE Technical failure: Hans Herrmann escaped with minor injuries after the brakes on his BRM failed at the end of the long straight at Avus, during the German Grand Prix in 1959.

OPPOSITE Fire: Niki Lauda crashed in 1976 after a suspected technical failure at the Nürburgring. His helmet was wrenched off, his face was badly burnt, he inhaled noxious fumes from the burning car and nearly lost his life. Through sheer willpower, and because he was still in with a chance of winning the World Championship that year, he was racing again in 2 months.

PREVIOUS PAGES Collision: Nelson Piquet and Riccardo Patrese in a moment of drama during the 1985 Monaco Grand Prix. Both survived.

all eyes and lenses on the winner's rostrum, away went the victor's traditional laurel wreath in case it obscured the sponsor's insignia on the driver's overalls.

Motor racing has become a multi-million dollar, global industry. At the top are the drivers, always the focus of attention; they are the ones with the rare skills, men set apart by danger. Once upon a time their reward was simply the glory of winning; later came modest financial prizes; now they are international superstars on a par with pop musicians and film stars.

An Indianapolis 500 winner today need never drive or work again. His share of the purse combined with sponsorship deals and personal appearances, makes him a multi-millionaire. Formula One and World Championship drivers are contracted to their teams for deals which run into millions of pounds for a season.

Why do drivers go on, risking their lives to win? The answer is deep inside them: they must be people for whom winning is all important. Coming second is no good, whatever the money.

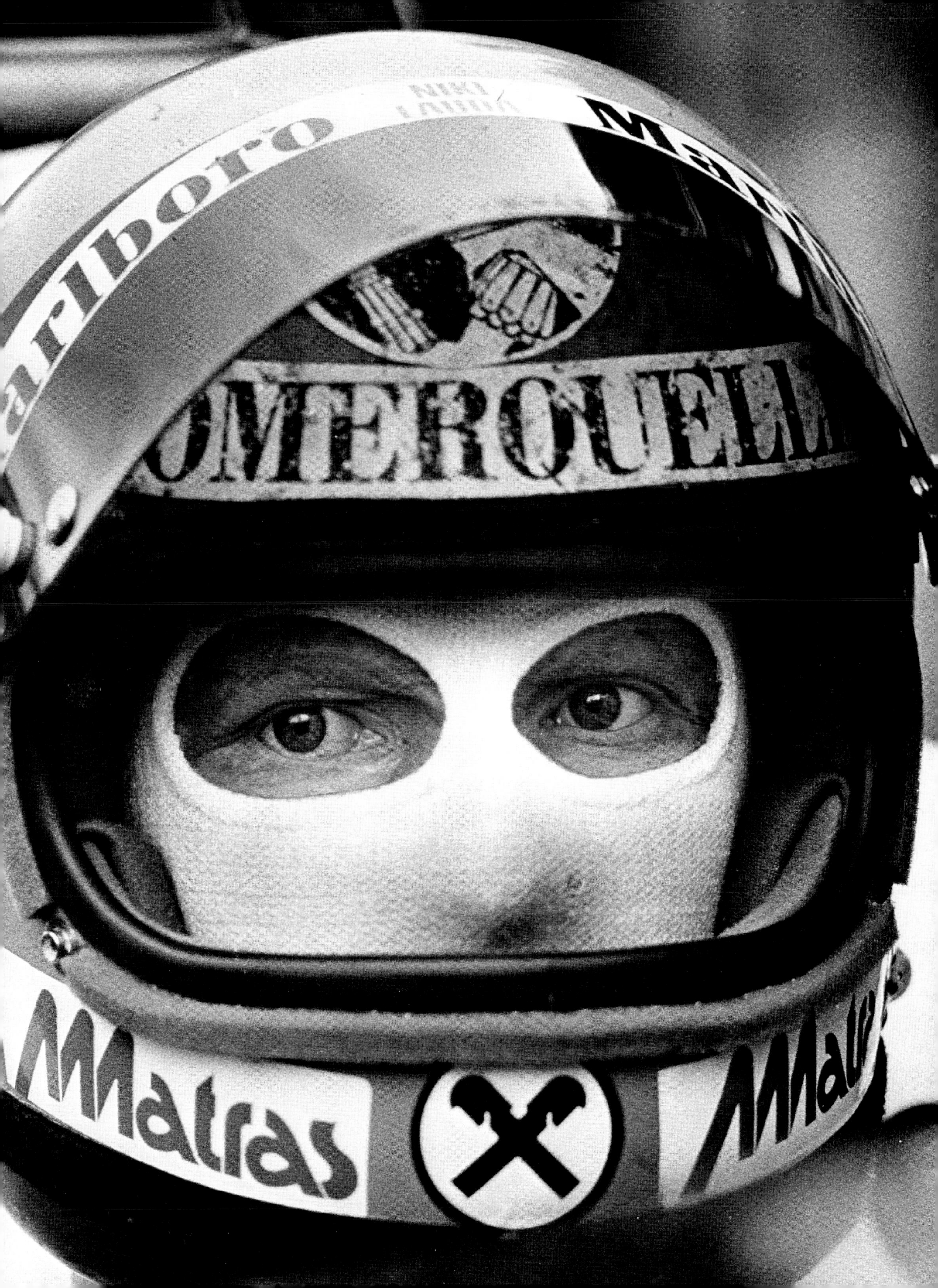

Matras

─ CHAPTER TWO ─
NATION SHALL RACE AGAINST NATION

Many a restless and ingenious mind was occupied during the second half of the nineteenth century in the quest to build a 'horseless carriage'. Steam, electricity, gas and kerosene were all used in experiments. However, it was the lightweight, internal combustion engine, burning petrol, which was developed during the 1880s, which led to the motor car as we know it today.

Karl Benz and Gottlieb Daimler, working independently in Germany, built the first practical motor cars, but they found real enthusiasm for their machines in France: the first recorded sale of a car was a Benz, to Emile Roger in Paris in March 1888. Two years later, at the Paris Exhibition of 1890, Daimler put his 1.5-bhp, four-wheeled *Stahlradwagen* (steel-wheeled car) on display. It was a great success and remained in France after the exhibition as a model for the French bicycle manufacturers, Peugeot, and the engineering firm, Panhard et Levassor. Both companies went on to use Daimler engines for their own cars and later built the engines under licence in France.

In the early 1890s, the motor car was seen more as a novelty than as a serious competitor for the horse or the railways, even in France. But Pierre Giffard, the owner of the Paris news magazine *Le Petit Journal*, was always eager to promote new ideas and in December 1893 his paper announced that it would organize a competitive event for '*voitures sans chevaux*' – horseless carriages. It was designed to publicize motor cars and encourage their use by showing that they were reliable and

LEFT **Emile Levassor (1843–97) – winner of the first motor race in history – is remembered with this statue in Paris.**

43

PARIS-ROUEN: 22 JULY 1894

Le Petit Journal announced the Paris–Rouen Trial on 19 December 1893. By 30 April the following year the magazine had received 102 entries. The imagination and enthusiasm with which the idea of the *'voitures sans chevaux'* had been grasped was amply illustrated by the range of ideas about how they were to be powered. Several entries listed the 'weight of the passengers' as the source of their motive power; a M. Rousselet listed 'gravity'; there were several 'automatic' cars and others were to be driven by electricity, hydraulics, compressed air, levers or pendulums. A majority were petrol or steam cars and the 21 which passed the qualifying runs round the streets of Paris and finished up on the start line at the Porte Maillot were all in these categories.

The event aroused great interest: schoolchildren were paraded on the side of the road, families took picnics,

Mr Gordon Bennett, a great American publisher, was in the crowd at the start and he sent one of his reporters to follow the cars on a bicycle. Four cars dropped out on the way, but the occupants were picked up by other contestants and everybody had arrived at Rouen by evening. Officially the times did not count, the winners were decided by a jury based on the practicability of the car as well as their performance. But unofficially they did. The fastest car was a huge de Dion steam tractor which carried its passengers in a carriage, like an articulated trailer. It covered the distance at an average speed of 11.6 mph, but was only awarded second prize because it needed a second man to stoke the engine. The next twelve were all petrol-driven cars, mostly Peugeots and Panhards, the two companies who shared first prize.

RIGHT TOP **M. Kraeutler** in his sixth-placed Peugeot in which he averaged 10.1 mph.

RIGHT CENTRE **M. Doriot**, who was third fastest at 11.1 mph, in his Peugeot Viz à Viz. The name was derived from the position of the driver and passengers who sat face to face, as in a horse-drawn carriage.

RIGHT **M. Michaud** driving through Mantes. He was ninth fastest in Peugeot No. 30 at 9.4 mph.

LEFT Peugeot's success in the Paris–Rouen Trial brought business to the company. This slightly later model of 1897 is preserved in running order by the company in its museum.

safe. A prize of 5000 francs was offered to the automobile which, in the opinion of the jury appointed by the paper, put up the best performance over the 78 miles between Paris and Rouen.

There were 102 entries which the organizers reduced to 21: 8 steam-powered, and 13 petrol-driven cars of which 12 were Daimler-engined Peugeots or Panhard-Levassors. The fastest was a de Dion steam tractor, but the jury decided that it was not a practical road vehicle. Instead, it awarded the prize jointly to the leading Peugeot, which had achieved an average speed of 11.5 mph, and to the Panhard which was close behind.

The Paris-Rouen Trial succeeded in its primary aim of stimulating interest in automobiles but, though competitive, it was not a race with all the glamour and excitement implied by raw competition between individual drivers and cars. It was clear that such an event would attract even more attention so, in 1895, a more ambitious event, this time indisputably a race, was organized from Paris to Bordeaux and back: 732 miles on dirt roads.

Among the starters at the Place d'Armes on 11 June 1895 was Emile Levassor, a director of Panhard-Levassor, driving the company's 'No. 5', a two-seater with solid rubber tyres and a 2-cylinder, 4-bhp engine. The race was expected to take four days, but Levassor was made of sterner stuff: he drove through the night, using candle-powered headlamps, and reached Bordeaux the following morning. He paused only briefly, then set off again, driving through a second night before arriving back in Paris at lunchtime on 13 June to wild enthusiasm from a huge crowd. It was an extraordinary feat of endurance for the man and his machine – 48 hours 48 minutes of virtually continuous driving at a bone-shaking average speed of 15 mph. However, the rules stated that the cars had to be four-seaters. His had only two, so he was denied the prize of 31,000 francs which went to M. Koechlin who came in 11 hours later in a Peugeot. The records show Koechlin as the victor, but it was Levassor who went down in history as the winner of the first motor race – and it was to him that the French authorities erected a statue overlooking the finishing line at the Porte Maillot in Paris.

The paintings of Gordon Crosby (1885–1957) are among the
most eloquent records of the pioneering years of motor racing:
Fernand Charron in a Panhard on the way to victory in the
Paris-Amsterdam race of 1898 – 889 miles in 33 hours 4 minutes.

LAST OF THE INTER-TOWN RACES

With speeds reaching 90–100 mph on open public roads, the French government was reluctant to sanction the Paris–Madrid race which the ACF planned for 1903. But public enthusiasm carried the day and it was scheduled for 24 May. Between two and three million people were reported to be along the route for the first day's racing to Bordeaux.

The first driver, Charles Jarrott driving a de Dietrich, was waved off at 3.45 a.m. in the gathering light. He had to drive at the crowd which parted at the last moment to let him through. By late morning the field was strung out over 100 miles kicking up huge clouds of dust.

The government's worst fears were realized. Two drivers, Lorraine Barrow from England and France's Marcel Renault, were killed; a riding mechanic and five spectators also died and many more were injured. The race was stopped, the cars were immobilized and towed to the railway station by horses.

Racing on open public roads was finished, but not before one of the classic drives of all time: Fernand Gabriel started well down the field at 82 but was second to arrive in Bordeaux, the unofficial winner with an average speed of 65.3 mph.

ABOVE **Gordon Crosby's** grim but heroic view of the Paris-Madrid race, painted 30 years after it took place.

BELOW **Marcel Renault** at speed in his 30-bhp Renault during the race; he was killed, but Vauthier, his riding mechanic, survived.

ABOVE RIGHT *Punch*'s view at the time was captioned 'The Race of Death', reflecting the view that such races should never have been permitted.

SOME CLASSIC INTER-TOWN RACES
1895 Paris–Bordeaux–Paris
      Emile Levassor (Panhard-Levassor)
1896 Paris–Marseilles–Paris
      Mayade (Panhard)
1898 Paris–Amsterdam–Paris
      Fernand Charron (Panhard)
1899 Paris–Bordeaux
      Fernand Charron (Panhard)
1899 Tour de France
      René de Knyff (Panhard)
1900 Paris–Lyons
      Fernand Charron (Panhard)
1900 Paris–Toulouse–Paris
      Levegh (Mors)
1901 Paris–Berlin
      Henri Fournier (Mors)
1902 Paris–Vienna
      Marcel Renault (Renault)
1903 Paris–Madrid
      Fernand Gabriel (Mors)

Levassor was back the following year for a 1063-mile race from Paris to Marseilles and back. South of Avignon, he swerved to avoid a dog, crashed and was taken to hospital with concussion. His works driver, M. Mayade, in an 8-bhp Panhard, went on to win. Panhard cars dominated inter-town events; as a result they were sought out by the best drivers, and kept on winning. Racing and, more important, coming first, boosted sales and the company flourished. Sadly, Levassor did not live to see the full measure of his success: he died on 14 April 1897, never having fully recovered from the effects of the accident.

Men like Levassor and Fernand Charron, his most successful driver, made France the undisputed capital of the sport. In November 1895 the Automobile Club de France (ACF) was formed to organize racing and the number of events grew steadily. In 1898, it was Paris to Amsterdam and back, in 1901 Paris to Berlin and in 1902 Paris to Vienna.

By contrast, road racing was banned in Britain. Not only that, the law required a man carrying a red flag to precede a moving car. Such restrictions stunted the British motor industry, and, after pressure from motorists, the rule was repealed in 1896. To celebrate, the Motor Car Club organized an event from London to Brighton on 14 November. Road racing on the French model was still banned so, to comply with the law, it was not technically a race. However, the drivers certainly treated it as one. The three fastest cars were all French: two tandem Bollée tricycles, driven by the brothers Léon and Camille Bollée, and a Panhard driven by the Earl of Winchilsea.

Sponsors and enthusiasts in other countries were equally eager to organize races. The *Chicago Times* sponsored the first one in the United States in November 1895. Only two cars made it to the start and only one, a Benz driven by Oscar Mueller, finished. The first event to be staged on a short track was also in America, at the Rhode Island State Fair at Cranston, RI, in September 1896. Eight drivers diced with each other over five laps of a 1-mile dirt track. An electrically powered Riker, driven by C. H. Whiting, won at an average speed of 24 mph.

THE FIRST INTERNATIONAL SERIES

The rules for the Gordon Bennett races introduced a strict formula based on weight rather than engine size: a minimum of 400 kg and a maximum of 1000 kg without driver, mechanic, fuel, oil and other consumables. The driver and mechanic had to weigh at least 60 kg each; weights were carried to make up the difference.

The cars were painted in national colours: originally blue for France, red for America, yellow for Belgium and white for Germany. An enduring legacy of the races, the colours lasted informally until advertising gradually superceded them in the 1960s.

BELOW **The Gordon Bennett Trophy, known in France as La Coupe Internationale.**

ABOVE RIGHT **Athy, Ireland 1903: Henri Farman (centre) and René de Knyff (right) in their 80-bhp Panhards. They were beaten by Camille Jenatzy in a 60-bhp Mercedes, the first of three defeats which the company was to inflict on French manufacturers before the First World War.**

RIGHT **Homburg, Germany 1904: revenge was sweet when Léon Théry recovered the trophy for France.**

By the turn of the century, it was clear that the motor car was going to be big business. Racing was part of that business. It provided an exciting sport for drivers and spectators, but its real value to the industry, and the reason for putting money into it, lay in the opportunities it created, to develop ever-better cars and to promote them to an ever-wider public. France's dominant position in the sport was of enormous value to its manufacturers.

In 1900, a challenge to that position came from an unexpected quarter. James Gordon Bennett, an American newspaper tycoon living in Paris, put up the cash and a beautiful trophy for a series of races designed to elevate motor racing to an organized international sport. In effect, however, these events challenged French dominance because of the rules Bennett imposed. He saw that the automobile industry in his native America was lagging behind those in Europe and his races were intended to encourage American manufacturers, as well as those in other countries, to compete with the French. Instead of being a competition between individual drivers and manufacturers, the series would be a contest between national teams, with cars painted in national colours.

Drivers and cars had to be selected and entered by the automobile club of each competing country and the winning country would stage the race the following year. The cars, including all components, had to be built in the country entering them. The innovation which most upset the French was that teams were limited to three cars. This restriction did not reflect their dominance of the sport: France could field several first-class teams while most other countries would have difficulty raising even one.

In deference to French expertise, the first race was organized by the ACF. The date was set for 14 June 1900; the route was from Paris to Lyons, a distance of 353 miles. There was a predictable row over which manufacturers should have the honour of representing France. A ballot was held to settle the matter, but when it produced three Panhard drivers and none from their great rivals, Mors, there was more than a whiff of scandal in the air.

Four countries entered teams: France was represented by the three Panhards, driven by Charron,

Napier was the first British car company to build racing cars. The 1908 car (ABOVE) was built for hill climbing; it was second fastest up the famous Shelsley Walsh Hill Climb in Worcestershire in 1911. The 6-cylinder engine (RIGHT) was 11.5 litres and produced around 60 bhp.

René de Knyff and Leonce Girardot, and America by two Wintons driven by Alexander Winton and Anthony Riker. There was a solitary Belgian entry, a Snoek-Bolide driven by Camille Jenatzy, and a Benz from Germany driven by Eugen Benz, the son of the pioneer. Benz and Riker pulled out before the start; Winton, Jenatzy and de Knyff retired after various difficulties, leaving the master, Charron, to win the first international motor race for France.

The only challenger to the French in 1901 was a lone British driver, Selwyn Edge, in a Napier. However, he pulled out because his tyres could not take the strain, leaving the two Panhards of Charron and Girardot and a Mors to battle it out between Paris and Bordeaux. Charron also had tyre problems and the Mors crashed, leaving Girardot to retain the trophy for France.

In 1902, the Gordon Bennett was run in conjunction with the Paris to Vienna race, but only over the 350 miles to Innsbruck. France and Britain entered teams. Girardot, Henri Fournier, Montague Graham-White and Arthur Callan dropped out early on, leaving de Knyff in a Panhard to fight it out with Edge in a Napier. Thirty miles short of Innsbruck, the Panhard broke down leaving the field to Edge. It was Britain's first real success in motor racing but it was a disaster for the French: Edge had shown that they could be beaten.

MOUNTAIN LEGEND

Motor racing, like most fields of human endeavour, has produced its legends. Among the most enduring was the Targa Florio which survived in the mountains of Sicily long after all other road races had been abandoned. Fifty-seven races were held, the last in 1973.

Such was its reputation that it became almost a rite of passage for successive generations of drivers. Most of the great names drove it at some point in their careers: Enzo Ferrari, Giuseppe Campari, Jules Goux and Antonio Ascari in the 1920s, Achille Varzi and Tazio Nuvolari in the 1930s, Juan Fangio and Stirling Moss in the 1950s and Graham Hill, Phil Hill and Dan Gurney in the 1960s.

But its unique ruggedness also made it a forum where the gifted amateur could shine, especially Italian drivers like Count Giovanni Lurani, and the Sicilian driver, Nino Vaccarella, who won in both 1965 and 1971.

ABOVE LEFT AND ABOVE The 1907 Targa Florio. Cars at the foot of the mountain course and Felice Nazzaro (above), a former Fiat apprentice who was Vincenzo Florio's personal mechanic and chauffeur, winning for his old firm.

LEFT The legendary quality of the Targa Florio found its way into Gordon Crosby's painting.

BELOW Early commercialism: the Tote at the Targa Florio in 1907.

There were two immediate consequences: international interest in the Gordon Bennett was rekindled, and the French were even more convinced that it had to be stopped. The following year, 1903, teams from Britain, France, America and Germany gathered at Athy in Ireland where Jenatzy, driving for Germany in a Mercedes, beat de Knyff, Henri Farman and Fernand Gabriel into second, third and fourth places.

When Germany staged the race in 1904, at Homburg near Frankfurt, the Kaiser was in attendance. At last the competition seemed to be realizing Gordon Bennett's hopes of becoming a major, international sporting event. America was not represented but there were 19 entries from Germany, Britain, Austria, Italy, France, Belgium and Switzerland. Some of the most illustrious names were there: Vincenzo Lancia from Italy, Fritz von Opel from Germany and Sidney Girling from Britain, all of whom went on to become prominent figures in their national motor industries. France had to hold an eliminating race to select its three entrants from a field of 29. Controversy surrounded the Mercedes ploy of entering one team to represent Germany and another for Austria. The race itself was an exciting battle between Léon Théry in a Richard-Brasier and Jenatzy in a Mercedes. Théry won and the trophy went back to France.

In 1905, in charge of organizing the event once more, the ACF tried to put an end to the Gordon Bennett races and replaced them with their new international Grand Prix, which was open to manufacturers rather than national teams. The club suggested that the two events be run in conjunction, but could not get agreement. It held an eliminating race in the Auvergne which proved much of their case against the Gordon Bennett: open to the whole French industry, it was an exciting contest between the best cars and many of the best drivers.

The Gordon Bennett was held over the same circuit on 5 July. Théry in a Richard-Brasier had a narrow victory over Italy's Felice Nazzaro in a Fiat, with Alessandro Cagno third in another Fiat. It was the last Gordon Bennett race. As the winners, the French were awarded the task of organizing the event the following year, but declined. It was open

RIGHT Renault's success in the Grand Prix of 1906 inspired William K. Vanderbilt to order three racing cars from the company for export to America. At 7.6 litres, the engines were smaller than the 13-litre Grand Prix cars, giving 45 bhp at 1200 revs, or just under 6 bhp/litre. The wheels were made of wood with detachable rims. This is one of the three, now preserved in Britain, where it appears at vintage events still topping 70 mph.

BELOW The four-speed Renault gearbox. To the right is a transmission brake operated by a foot pedal, in addition to the hand, or 'side', brake which operated on the rear wheels only.

to the Italian Club, whose driver had come second, to do so, but they also refused and the series lapsed. The Gordon Bennett's contribution had been to provide both a framework and a forum for international motor racing. But in setting national ideals above the commercial needs of manufacturers and the individual needs of drivers it was contrary to the dynamics of motor racing.

The ACF could control the sport in France, but could not stop other countries organizing events. America never won the Gordon Bennett so none of the races had been held there. It was another newspaper publisher, William K. Vanderbilt, who organized a cup in his name to put the United States on the international motor-racing circuit. The Vanderbilt Cup was open to international drivers and

cars but the rules stated that the first two races had to be held in America, then after that in the country of the winner. The first was held on Long Island on 8 October 1904. The winner was an American, George Heath, but he was driving a Panhard. The spectators were so excited they invaded the track at the finish.

In Europe, Italy was challenging France as a builder of racing cars: in the last Gordon Bennett race, two Fiats driven by Nazzaro and Cagno, had come second and third. What Italy needed was a man of vision and wealth to organize a major event. It found one, not in a newspaper publisher, but in the son of a wealthy Palermo merchant. Count Vincenzo Florio had taken part in several races, including the ill-fated 1903 Paris-Madrid. In 1904, he started organizing events including the Coppa Florio, a 231-mile road race, starting in the northern Italian town of Brescia.

But what Florio wanted was a spectacular contest to match the forthcoming Grand Prix in France. To attract the top drivers, he commissioned an ornate solid-gold plate from craftsmen in Paris. To provide a challenge worthy of the trophy, he surveyed his native Sicily for a supremely demanding course. He settled on a 92-mile circuit in the Madonie mountains on the north coast, which started alongside the beach at Campofelice, then wound its way to a high point of over 3600 ft, before descending again, in a severe test of brakes, to sea level. Drivers would be pitting their cars against some of the toughest roads and harshest geography in Europe, a test of courage, stamina and determination on the part of the driver and of structural integrity in the car. There were ten starters in the race on 5 May 1906 and the event was as gruelling as Florio had imagined it would be. Some cars simply disintegrated under the strain, but six made it to the end led by Cagno in an Itala, with Ettore Graziani second in another.

The first Targa Florio was run just before the motor-racing world turned its attention to the event the ACF hoped would become the blue riband of the sport: the first Grand Prix at Le Mans on 26/27 June 1906. It was run over two days, six laps each day round a 64-mile circuit totalling 768 miles. The

RIGHT The winning car: the 1906 Grand Prix Renault had a 4-cylinder, 12.9-litre engine which developed 90 bhp at 1200 rpm or 6.97 bhp/litre; there were three gears, and the drive was through a shaft to the rear axle rather than the chain drive which was in more common use at the time. Its maximum speed was 103 mph.

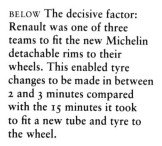

BELOW The decisive factor: Renault was one of three teams to fit the new Michelin detachable rims to their wheels. This enabled tyre changes to be made in between 2 and 3 minutes compared with the 15 minutes it took to fit a new tube and tyre to the wheel.

LE MANS 1906: BIRTHPLACE OF THE GRAND PRIX

Le Mans is a name synonymous with motor racing. Like Indianapolis, it is one of the few remaining places to have a continuous link with the sport going back to the earliest times. It is better known for the 24-hour sports car race, but in 1906 it was the site of the first Grand Prix. The circuit has changed over the years but in 1906 the event was run over the Circuit de la Sarthe, an 80-mile-long course to the west of the town; the circuit was diverted round some of the built-up areas.

A feature of Le Mans was the long, fast straights covered in small, sharp stones. Exhaust pipes had to be directed upwards to stop these adding to the dust cloud. Drivers protected their eyes with goggles and their faces with masks but with speeds of 100 mph commonplace, their cheeks would be puffed up and bleeding from the flying debris after a day's racing. The second Renault driver in the 1906 Grand Prix, J. Edmond, had to retire when a stone smashed his goggles and went into his eye.

LEFT The winning driver: François Szisz, born in Hungary, made his career as a racing driver in France.

LEFT AND ABOVE **Peking to Paris 1907, the ultimate inter-town race: 9500 miles across Asia and Europe. This epic event was sponsored by the newspaper** *Le Matin* **and attracted enormous interest. The winner was the Italian Prince Scipione Borghese driving a specially prepared Itala. He was accompanied by a journalist, Luigi Barzini, and a mechanic, Ettore Guizzardi.**

There were four entries and they set out from Peking on 10 June 1907. The Italians arrived in Paris exactly two months later on 10 August (above); the second car home was a de Dion which arrived two months after that. No other cars finished.

cars were locked up overnight in a paddock then released the following day, to restart with the same time-intervals at which they had finished the previous day. Each manufacturer was allowed a team of three cars. The field showed why French manufacturers had been so frustrated by the Gordon Bennett races: of the 12 teams entered, nine were French. Fiat and Itala represented Italy and Mercedes Germany. The French teams were a *Who's Who* of the industry: Panhard, Clement-Bayard, Hotchkiss, Gobron-Brillie, de Dietrich, Renault, Darracq, Richard-Brasier and Gregoire.

François Szisz, Louis Renault's riding mechanic in the 1903 Paris-Madrid, was Renault's leading driver and took an early lead. He battled for a time with the faster 105-bhp Richard-Brasiers but, on a surface which was punishing to everybody's tyres, Renault's detachable rims gave Szisz a crucial advantage. Driving consistently and fast, he held his lead for the rest of the 2 days, winning by 32 minutes from Nazzaro. The first Grand Prix had gone to France. But for the first time, the strength of the Italian industry was evident, posing a challenge to French manufacturers.

On 22 April 1907 the Targa Florio attracted a field of 49 cars and the scene was set for a classic battle between the Italians and the French. Lancia took an early lead in a Fiat with a host of Italian cars and drivers close behind. On the second lap Nazzaro, in another Fiat, went into the lead and a fierce duel developed between him and Louis Wagner in a Darracq. Under pressure, Wagner's half shaft broke on the last lap and the Italians romped home: Nazzaro, then Lancia, followed by Maurice Fabry in an Itala. Nazzaro's car had a 7-litre engine, evidence of a trend towards smaller and more efficient engines.

ABOVE LEFT Road racing on the European model came to America in 1904: the Vanderbilt Cup was held on Long Island in October and drew a huge crowd. The winning driver was George Heath, an American, but his car was French, a Panhard. Second was Albert Clement in a Clement-Bayard. American cars – a Pope Toledo and a Packard – would have been next, had the crowd not invaded the track.

LEFT Arthur Duray came third in the Vanderbilt Cup of 1906 in a de Dietrich after a dramatic incident when he had to help his mechanic hold on to a spare tyre which had come loose. European drivers and cars filled the first seven places in the race which was badly policed and suffered several track invasions. The American cars were fitted with studded tyres which were unsuitable for the wet conditions.

ABOVE Eddie Pullen losing a wheel from his Mercer at Death Curve during the 1914 Vanderbilt Cup at Santa Monica, California. American cars were dominant in this event and in the American Grand Prize that year. But road racing was in decline, overshadowed by track events, in particular, the Indianapolis 500. Pullen won the American Grand Prize in 1914, the first American to do so in an American car.

On 13 June 1907, the racing world gathered in the Taunus forest in the presence of Kaiser Wilhelm II for the German Automobile Club's 'Kaiserpreis', Germany's debut on the international racing stage. The trophy had the likeness of the Emperor etched on to it. There was a huge entry: 78 cars built to an 8-litre formula which had been set to encourage smaller engines. The event was run over two days, with two heats and a final. Lancia won the first heat; Nazzaro won the second and went on to win the race.

The battle between France and Italy reached a climax that year at the Grand Prix which was held at Dieppe. The French predominated with 11 teams to one each from Belgium, Italy, Britain, America and Germany. The ACF introduced a formula

LEFT Road racing was banned on the British mainland, but from 1905 the Tourist Trophy races were held on the Isle of Man. Humber built three cars for the 1914 TT, none of which finished the race. The one shown here is still driven in Vintage Sports Car Club events today.

ABOVE The Humber's 3.2-litre, double overhead camshaft engine developed 110 bhp at 3000 revs; 34 bhp/litre. It can still reach 90 mph over a standing kilometre.

based on fuel consumption rather than engine size: 30 litres per 100 km. The rules also introduced a touch of nationalism, requiring cars to carry national racing colours again. The year belonged to Nazzaro, Fiat and Italy: the Italian driver won by seven minutes after a battle with Szisz in the Renault. French dominance had been badly cracked and French pride was severely dented.

If 1907 was a bad year for France, 1908 was worse. The Grand Prix formula now limited piston area to 117 sq. in., coupled with a minimum weight of 1100 kg to stop designers making their cars dangerously light. The course was once again at Dieppe. Otto Salzer for Mercedes took an early lead which then changed hands between Nazzaro and Wagner for Fiat and Victor Hemery for Benz, until halfway through the race when the German driver Christian Lautenschlager took over in his 13.5-litre Mercedes. By steady driving he held it to the finish, with Benz's men second and third. It was a triumph for Germany.

ABOVE Ernest Henry, the enigmatic Swiss draughtsman and designer who was behind the revolutionary double overhead camshaft engine.

LEFT A famous René Vincent poster of one of the landmarks in the development of the racing car: the Peugeot.

BELOW A later Henry-designed engine in a post-First-World-War Ballot. The basic principles of double overhead camshafts, four valves per cylinder and hemispherical combustion chamber, have guided high-performance engine design to the present day.

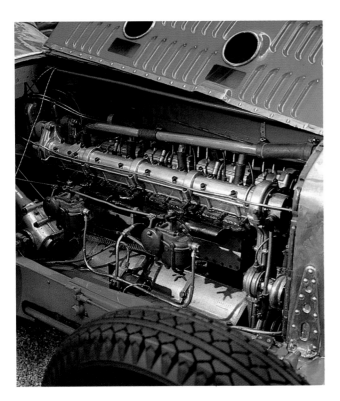

The German victory was the last straw for the French manufacturers. The high cost of racing had been justified in the past by the publicity which came from winning. Now they were losing and the cost of building a new car each year was going up. In addition, the Grand Prix car had developed into a monster, far removed from the touring cars the manufacturers were supposed to promote. On top of that, Europe went into recession in 1908. National humiliation might pass, but when economics took a firm grip on events, the French industry collectively decided to pull out of Grand Prix racing. The ACF tried to organize one for 1909, but the industry boycott held firm and it was cancelled.

In the absence of the Grand Prix, drivers looked across the Atlantic where, in addition to the Vanderbilt Cup, a new race, the American Grand Prize, was held at Savannah in November 1908. A 25-mile road circuit had been prepared using convict labour and provided a superb forum for European drivers and their cars which were still well in advance of those in the United States: Wagner won in a Fiat, followed by Hemery in a Benz and Nazzaro in a Fiat. In 1910, the Grand Prize had its first American winner, David Bruce-Brown, this time in a Benz. He repeated his success in 1911 in a Fiat.

In Europe, with Grand Prix racing apparently on its deathbed, drivers and spectators turned to events for smaller cars, known as 'voiturettes', to fill the vacuum. These had originally been some of the lightest of the lighter cars that had been raced since the turn of the century, but gradually most of the smaller cars became known collectively by this name. In the early days, there was no major prize for voiturette racing but in 1905 *L'Auto* magazine inaugurated the Coupe des Voiturettes. The first event was disappointing, but in 1906 the race attracted a field of 22. The winner was Georges Sizaire in a Sizaire-Naudin; second was Menart Lucas in a Delage, followed by two Lion-Peugeots driven by Cesare Giuppone and Jules Goux.

In 1907, voiturette racing spread to Italy, one race being held over the Targa Florio circuit. The winner was Louis Naudin, the other half of the Sizaire-Naudin partnership. In the Coupe des Voiturettes that year it was Sizaire's turn to win, with

BELOW Boillot in a Lion-Peugeot voiturette in 1908. He became a fighter pilot in the First World War and was killed in combat over Verdun in 1916.

ABOVE Georges Boillot makes a pit stop during the race.

RIGHT A poster celebrating the return of Grand Prix racing in 1912.

DIEPPE 1912: A WATERSHED RACE

The 1912 Grand Prix was held at Dieppe over 956 miles spread over two days. The favourites were the 14.1-litre Fiats, powerful cars from an earlier age which had been doing well in America. The Peugeots were only a little over half the size at 7.6 litres.

On the first lap, David Bruce-Brown driving for Fiat took the lead, with Georges Boillot second in a Peugeot. Then Louis Wagner in another Fiat passed Boillot and Paul Zuccarelli and Jules Goux both dropped out leaving Boillot alone with the two big Fiats. At the end of the first day Bruce-Brown was leading Boillot by 2 minutes.

On the second day, they started off at intervals equivalent to their finishing position the previous day. On lap 15 disaster struck Bruce-Brown: his fuel pipe broke and though he refuelled, in so doing he infringed the rules. He was disqualified leaving the race to Boillot, a lucky win but one which accelerated the trend towards smaller engines.

BELOW **Boillot, his devoted mechanic Charles Prévost and their revolutionary 7.6-litre Peugeot on their way to** victory in 1912. The Peugeot was the first car to achieve over 20 bhp/litre.

Naudin second and Goux third for Lion-Peugeot. The ACF, seeing the attraction of voiturette racing, organized a Grand Prix des Voiturettes on the day before the 1908 Grand Prix. Albert Guyot won in a Delage, followed by Naudin, then two Lion-Peugeots driven by Goux and Georges Boillot. Later the same year in the Coupe des Voiturettes it was Naudin, Sizaire and then Goux. In the Targa Florio of 1910, so few big cars entered that Florio ran the voiturettes with them. They started behind the big cars, but were an hour ahead by the end, a triumph for Peugeot with Boillot first, then Giuppone, then Goux.

Later that year, in the Coupe des Voiturettes, Peugeot received two setbacks: Giuppone was killed in practice at Boulogne and in the race, Paul Zuccarelli, driving a Hispano-Suiza, beat Goux into second place with another Hispano third. The secret of Hispano's success lay in its engine. The voiturette formula, based on the diameter of the cylinder, had produced some outlandishly tall, 1- and 2-cylinder engines which made the cars quite unstable and difficult to handle as a result, a factor which had probably contributed to Giuppone's death. Zuccarelli's Hispano had a much more compact 4-cylinder engine which made the car much easier to handle than Goux's 2-cylinder Peugeot, even though the latter was faster.

Giuppone's death left a gap in the Lion-Peugeot team and Boillot and Goux were keen to have Zuccarelli and his ideas for new engines at Peugeot, especially because the formula for 1911 was changed to a maximum of 3 litres which gave wider scope for new designs. Boillot, Goux and Zuccarelli hatched a plan to build a completely new, high-performance engine and persuaded Robert Peugeot to let them have a free hand in its design. He gave them a fixed sum of money and told them to get on with it. They took on Ernest Henry, a Swiss draughtsman, who had also spent some time at Hispano. Peugeot's own design engineers, with years of training behind them, were outraged and christened the three drivers the 'Charlatans'. The trio came up with a synthesis of ideas for high-performance engines which revolutionized racing: the first double overhead camshaft engine.

In 1912, the ACF announced that it would reinstate the Grand Prix. Peugeot set its sights on winning the race with its new engine, its three talented drivers and its voiturette experience. The event was a gripping battle between the Peugeots and two giant Fiats driven by Bruce-Brown and Wagner. Boillot won after Bruce-Brown retired with mechanical problems.

It was a lucky win, but the Peugeots had shown the way ahead. Goux went to America and won a stunning victory for the company in the Indianapolis 500. For the 1913 season in Europe, Peugeot reduced the engine size to 5.6 litres, while boosting its output to around 30 bhp/litre. For the 1913 Grand Prix, Peugeot was sadly without Zuccarelli who had been killed in practice, but Boillot won convincingly with Goux second. Thanks to Peugeot and the Charlatans, France looked as if they were back on top. The double overhead camshaft engine set the trend and when the racing world gathered at Lyons for the 1914 Grand Prix virtually all the 41 cars had them.

The date was 4 July 1914, just six days after the assassination of Archduke Ferdinand in Sarajevo. Europe was simmering on the brink of war. Over 300,000 people were out around the 23-mile circuit. The atmosphere was tense in anticipation of personal, technical and national rivalries. Mercedes had entered a strong and meticulously prepared team with Lautenschlager, the man who had humiliated the French in 1908, backed up by Max Sailer, Salzer and Wagner. French hopes rested on Peugeot represented by Boillot, Goux and Victor Rigal in the new L45 car. The Mercedes cars were fractionally more powerful, but their handling was far superior and their drivers raced as a team using carefully planned tactics. The Germans finished first, second and third with Lautenschlager, Wagner and Salzer; Goux was fourth and Rigal seventh. France was humiliated again.

So the pioneering age of motor racing ended with arguably the greatest race so far. It also ended on a note of high and poignant drama: there was no applause for the German victors at Lyons and less than a month later Germany and France were at war.

RIGHT The 1914 Grand Prix Mercedes: shaft-driven, rear-wheel brakes only; 4.5-litre DOHC engine developed 115 bhp at 3200 rpm; 25.8 bhp/litre.

BELOW Lautenschlager pursued by Jules Goux on the downhill stretch towards Les Sept Chemins corner. Goux tried to unsettle Lautenschlager by breaking late, tempting the German driver into making a mistake. Lautenschlager let him pass, then used his extra power to overtake the Peugeot on the straight. Goux finished fourth after the three Mercedes.

LYONS 1914: THE GREATEST GRAND PRIX

It was a race of tactics: Max Sailer took an early lead and set a furious pace, forcing the Peugeots to go flat out. After five laps his Mercedes broke under the strain but he had done his job: he had stretched Georges Boillot and Jules Goux to their limits and demonstrated the superiority of the German cars.

Lautenschlager, who had started five minutes behind Boillot, had moved up steadily and was only a minute behind him when Sailer retired. Goux was just behind Lautenschlager followed by Louis Wagner and Otto Salzer. On the 18th lap Lautenschlager applied pressure to Boillot and took over the lead, pulling a minute ahead of him. Boillot drove the race of his life, trying all he knew, but the car had given everything it could and on the last lap the engine gave up, leaving Lautenschlager superbly poised to win.

LEFT Christian Lautenschlager was a company driver for Daimler for whom he had worked since 1900; he continued to race after the First World War.

—CHAPTER THREE—
DESIGNER DECADE

In November 1918, Europe was a dislocated continent: a generation of young men had been lost and a way of life had disappeared. National economies, harnessed for arms production, were preoccupied by reverting to peacetime conditions; motor racing was not high on the list of priorities. France and Germany, the two foremost racing nations in 1914, were the two countries most exhausted in manpower and resources.

America, where the top-class events had continued until the United States came into the First World War in 1917, had not been so traumatized. Racing was a profitable business and at Indianapolis Carl Fisher, the financial brains behind the speedway, set 30 May 1919 as the date to start racing again. He was keen to attract European entries to add to the lustre of the first race.

One man who wanted to be there was the French driver, René Thomas. In May 1914, driving a Delage, he had led a procession of European cars to victory at Indianapolis in an emphatic demonstration of Europe's superiority in design and engineering: Leon Duray was second in a Peugeot, Albert Guyot third in another Delage and Jules Goux fourth in another Peugeot. In fifth place was the first all-American combination of Barney Oldfield in a Stutz. Thomas had not forgotten the sweetness of that victory during the war and in 1918 he was determined to repeat it.

LEFT Art or engineering: the competitive cars of the 1920s were designed and built to win, but in the relentless pursuit of that function designers found a form, a beauty even, which few other periods matched. Some of the best-looking cars were also the most successful: a 4.5-litre, supercharged 'Blower' Bentley from 1930, the fourth year in succession that the company won the 24-hour race at Le Mans.

He wanted a new car for the race and his first step was to approach Ernest Henry, the man behind the revolutionary pre-war Peugeot engines. Together they went to see Ernest Ballot, a French engine manufacturer, who planned to build passenger cars. Convinced that racing would publicize his cars, Ballot signed a contract on Christmas Eve 1918 with René Thomas as driver and Ernest Henry as engine designer.

One important legacy of the war to motor racing was increased engine power. In the struggle for advantage in the air, pilots constantly needed more power and enormous effort had been put into developing increasingly powerful aero-engines. Ettore Bugatti, an Italian, had moved to France long before 1914 and established a motor-car factory at Molsheim near Strasbourg. He was drawn into aircraft engine development after the factory was seized by the Germans. His brainchild was a 24-litre, 16-cylinder aircraft engine with two parallel banks of 8 in-line cylinders. The war ended before it could go into production, but its development had been a valuable proving ground for ideas, particularly the 8 in-line cylinder configuration. Henry had been part of Bugatti's team and he now put his 'straight-eight' expertise to good use in a new 5-litre, double overhead camshaft engine.

Having committed himself to the project, Ballot did not hold back on the resources: he invested £30,000 to build four cars for Indianapolis and took on Guyot, Paul Bablot and Louis Wagner to complete the driving team. To meet the deadline for the race, the new cars had to be designed and built from scratch in 102 days.

Henry was not the only designer to have worked on the Bugatti aero-engine. The United States Government had selected it for further development in America where it was known as the Bugatti-King after the engineer in charge, Charles King. (King had driven in the first motor race in America in 1895.) Testing and production were carried out at the Duesenberg Motor Company engine plant at Elizabeth, New Jersey.

Frederick and August Duesenberg had built racing cars before the war and wanted to use the

ABOVE **Barney Oldfield** (centre), **Henry Ford** (right) and **Jules Goux** (extreme left) at the 1921 Indianapolis 500.

BELOW **Tommy Milton** (driver, right) with **Jimmy** Murphy (mechanic, left) at the 1919 Indianapolis, in the only Duesenberg to start. Milton became the first man to win the Indianapolis 500 twice. Murphy was the first American to win the French Grand Prix.

AMERICAN CHAMPIONS

Many of the most successful cars in the United States during the years of the First World War were European Grand Prix models, particularly the 1914 Grand Prix Peugeots and Mercedes. The 1915 Vanderbilt Cup and the American Grand Prize were won by Dario Resta in a Peugeot. Howard Wilcox won the Vanderbilt in 1916 for the same company. The last American Grand Prize was run at Santa Monica, California, on 18 November 1916. It was also the last event in that year's American National Championship, which both Resta and Johnnie Aitken could still win. Aitken's Peugeot broke down on the first lap. Resta then dropped out with ignition problems. Two laps later, Aitken took over Wilcox's Peugeot, hoping to finish the race and beat Resta for the championship, whereupon Resta tried to buy Earl Cooper's Stutz which was lying second. Cooper declined to sell. Aitken went on to win, but the rules forbade a change of driver and Resta won the championship after all.

The United States National Championship races were mainly run over dirt tracks, many of them built for horse racing at State Fairs, and on board speedways, 1 to 2-miles long, pure 'speedbowls' made of wood with a slope of 45 degrees. They were incredibly fast and very dangerous: at the inaugural meeting of the Uniontown Pennsylvania on 2 December 1916 three drivers were killed in the 100-mile race, which was won by Louis Chevrolet. But these tracks were the breeding grounds of the racing stars of post-war America.

LEFT **Ralph de Palma, an Italo-American, won the 1915 Indianapolis 500 in a 1914 Grand Prix Mercedes, just ahead of Dario Resta in a 1914 Peugeot. In 1916, Resta won in the Peugeot – de Palma was not there in the Mercedes. In the same year, Resta drove his Peugeot to victory in the Chicago 300 against de Palma in his Mercedes.**

BELOW LEFT **Dario Resta.**

BELOW **'Howdy' Wilcox.**

sport to publicize their name in the passenger-car market. They were also determined to put their experience with the Bugatti-King engine, and the test facilities which had been paid for by the Government, to good use.

The 1919 Indianapolis 500 was the first post-war classic. Cars of up to 5 litres were permitted to race and this attracted a field which included older, familiar cars as well as new challengers. The 'Indianapolis' Ballots were shipped to America from Le Havre on 20 April 1919. When they arrived for testing, they were found to be overgeared and had to have smaller wheels fitted, but they were capable of 118 mph. The Duesenbergs had been prepared in great haste and only one, driven by the American driver Tommy Milton, made it to the starting grid. It had a straight eight engine with a single overhead camshaft. The Chevrolet brothers, Louis and Gaston, were driving Frontenacs designed by themselves, and Ralph de Palma drove a Packard. There were also five pre-war Peugeots including three 4.5-litre, 1914 Grand Prix cars driven by Goux and the American drivers Howard Wilcox and Art Klein.

ABOVE **After the First World War there was a rush to build board speedways and cash in on the popularity of oval-track racing. Jimmy Murphy won the 200-mile inaugural race at the Fresno, California, track in October 1920 in a Duesenberg. Another Duesenberg was second.**

ABOVE RIGHT **The Kansas City Speedway opened in 1922. A million feet of 4 × 2 in. timber was used in its construction at a cost of $500,000. The early stages of the inaugural race on 17 September were dominated by the Duesenberg team, seen here in first, second and third place, but the event was won by Tommy Milton in a Miller Special. After two years, the track started breaking up; the last race was held on Independence Day 1924.**

Thomas gave the Ballot team a good start by setting the fastest qualifying lap with a record-breaking 104.7 mph. This gave him 'pole position', the most advantageous place on the starting grid. (Unlike European races, the cars all started together, their position on the grid determined by their qualifying times.) In spite of Thomas's initial advantage, the first half of the race was an all-American battle between de Palma and Gaston Chevrolet. The Duesenberg engine gave Milton trouble and he retired. At the halfway point, Louis Chevrolet was in the lead but it was not to last: 'Howdy' Wilcox came through in the 1914 Peugeot

and managed to hold the lead to the end. Second was Ed Hearne in a Durant/Stutz and Goux was third in another Peugeot. It was a triumph for the older, 4-cylinder cars, but the Ballots were not disgraced: Guyot brought his in fourth and Thomas was in 11th place.

The formula for the 1920 Indianapolis was set at 3 litres. Ballot persevered with the 8-cylinder engine and Thomas was back with a new car. De Palma drove another. Two star drivers, Milton and Jimmy Murphy, were driving new 8-cylinder, 3-litre Duesenbergs. For most of the race, it looked as though Ballot would triumph with de Palma leading for 186 of the 200 laps. Then a magneto problem slowed him down, letting Gaston Chevrolet through to win for America in a 4-cylinder Monroe. Thomas was second for Ballot with Milton third followed by Murphy. De Palma was fifth in the other Ballot and set the fastest lap at 99.15 mph; Hearne was sixth in another Duesenberg. Although a 4-cylinder car had won, straight eight engines had shown the way ahead.

The first classic race in Europe after the war was the Targa Florio held on 23 November 1919.

The Targa was run under 'Formula Libre' rules which put no restriction on engine size. The result was a grand mixture of works cars and private entries, mostly Italian. Many of the drivers became the central figures of the sport in the post-war racing world. André Boillot, brother of Georges, was there in a privately entered Peugeot. Giuseppe Campari was driving for Alfa Romeo. Antonio Ascari, a car dealer, had privately entered a 1914 Grand Prix Fiat which he had bought during the war. Enzo Ferrari drove a CMN (Costruzioni Meccaniche Nazionali) and Thomas was there in his Indianapolis Ballot.

Ascari crashed and the race became a battle between Boillot and Thomas. The latter led for much of the race, but by the time they reached the last lap Boillot was ahead. In an attempt to regain the lead, Thomas crashed. Then Boillot did the same, into the grandstand near the finish, and broke the rules by reversing. He had to drive back to the point where he had crashed and re-cross the finishing line, but he won – then he collapsed over the wheel, crying out '_C'est pour La France._'

By 1921, France was ready to mount a Grand Prix again and European racing was back in full swing. The Automobile Club de France chose Le Mans and adopted the 3-litre Indianapolis formula, partly in an attempt to attract entries from America. Duesenberg rose to the challenge and sent a team of four cars driven by Murphy, André Dubonnet, Joe Boyer and Guyot. At the 1921 Indianapolis 500, two months previously, Milton, driving a straight eight Frontenac, had just beaten Duesenberg into second place although the American cars also came in fourth, sixth and eighth.

Like the Duesenberg entries, the four Ballot cars were driven by a mixture of French and American drivers: de Palma, Jean Chassagne, Wagner and Goux. Sunbeam entered a team that included the British drivers and Brooklands stars, Henry Segrave and Kenelm Lee Guinness, and the Frenchmen André Boillot and Thomas. Fiat's new 8-cylinder Tipo 802 was held up at the factory because of industrial action. All the entries were 3-litre straight eights except for Goux's 2-litre Peugeot.

Murphy crashed in practice and came to the start line swathed in bandages. The early battle was between Ballot and Duesenberg: on the first lap de Palma and Boyer fought it out before Murphy came through to take the lead. Chassagne moved ahead of him after a pit stop, but was forced to retire with a split fuel tank on the 17th lap. Murphy took the lead again. On the last lap, his radiator was damaged, probably by a flying stone. The engine boiled and he had to change a wheel, but he struggled on, steaming, and lost another tyre before crossing the line to win. Second was de Palma for Ballot; third was Goux for Peugeot with Dubonnet fourth for Duesenberg.

THE 1921 FRENCH GRAND PRIX

RIGHT ABOVE Skill: consistent driving by Jimmy Murphy on the rough and stony Le Mans circuit gave him the lead.

RIGHT Murphy about to pass Ralph de Palma: the 2964 cc Duesenberg produced 117 bhp at 4250 rpm; 39.47 bhp/litre. The 2973-cc Ballot produced 107 bhp at 3800 rpm; 35.99 bhp/litre.

FAR RIGHT Jubilation: Murphy's riding mechanic, Ernie Olson, signals victory. The Duesenberg was the first car to enter a Grand Prix with four-wheel, hydraulically operated brakes, enabling Murphy to use shorter braking distances.

LEFT A man and his engine: Harry Miller with the 91 cu. in. (1.5-litre), 8-cylinder, supercharged engine which dominated American racing during the late 1920s: Miller's cars comprised three-quarters of the starters in the 1926 Indianapolis, and his ideas influenced racing engine design in America until the late 1970s. He was born in Wisconsin in 1875, left school at 14 to work as a machinist and transformed the look of racing cars in the 1920s. He died of a heart attack in 1943.

ABOVE A man and his car: Jimmy Murphy in a Miller 122 at the start of the 2-litre formula in 1923. Murphy went on to win the American National Championship the following year. Sadly, it was posthumous. On 15 September 1924 he crashed into the fencing at the Syracuse dirt track and was killed. His coffin was taken back to California in a train; crowds turned out at every stop to pay their respects.

ABOVE RIGHT Record breaker: British driver Ernest Eldridge at the Brickyard in a Miller 91. He used one to break world records at 5 km, 5 miles and 10 km at Montlhéry in France.

An American driver, driving an American car, had won the French Grand Prix, the high point of American racing in the international field. It was too much for Ballot, who pulled out to concentrate on the domestic market; Henry went to Sunbeam. But such transatlantic battles did not flourish. In Europe the sport continued in the tradition of road racing while America concentrated more and more on tracks. Indianapolis was the great annual event, but oval-track racing was steadily spreading throughout the country at local 'board speedways'.

This type of racing had started in 1910 at Pleya del Rey in California. The tracks were between 1 and 2 miles long and built entirely out of wood. Speed was of the essence and owners vied with

each other to promote themselves as providing the fastest circuits. In the early 1920s, entrepreneurs from Beverley Hills in California to Atlantic City, New Jersey, started building speedways. They attracted huge paying crowds and the Amerian National Championships were run on them. Racing was strictly for cash prizes, with total purses ranging between $15,000 and $20,000 shared between the first 10 or 12 places. These events demanded a different type of car from road racing, with good stability and powerful, reliable engines which could sustain high speeds over several hours. Brakes and gearboxes, vital in road events, were of less importance.

On his return from France in 1921, Murphy decided to capitalize on his new fame as Grand Prix winner on the board speedways. To do so, he needed a more powerful car. He went to Los Angeles, to Harry Miller, a carburettor manufacturer and a specialist designer whose engines were ideal for the American circuits.

Miller had supplied the carburettors for the Bugatti-King aero-engine, and, indeed, for Murphy's winning Duesenberg. He was a perfectionist. His Los Angeles factory became a centre of excellence in race engineering and in 1921 he had a superb 3-litre, straight eight engine to offer Murphy: the Miller 183. (The designation 183 was its cubic-inch capacity, the equivalent of 3 litres.) Murphy installed the engine in his Duesenberg chassis for the 1922 Indianapolis 500. Duesenberg took eight out of the first 10 places, but it was Murphy who won the event with his Miller engine. He went on to win the American National Championship that year on the speedways.

Miller was a brilliant, intuitive designer. He did not start out with a mass of stress calculations, but imagined the part he wanted and how it would fit into the whole. To put his ideas into practice, he surrounded himself with the right people, in particular Leo Goosen, an expert draughtsman and Fred Offenhauser, a talented machinist.

In 1923, the formula for Indianapolis changed to 2 litres and riding mechanics were excluded. The way was clear for a pure, single-seat car dedicated solely to racing. Miller was the first to build one. The Miller 122 set the look of racing cars for years to come: a slim body with a wheel at each corner, a machine whose function – speed – was clear, but one which was also superbly finished, reliable and powerful.

There were seven Miller 122s in the 1923 Indianapolis 500. Five were in a team sponsored by Cliff Durant, the son of the founder of General Motors, and two raced as HCS Specials, called after their sponsor, Harry C. Stutz, who wanted to publicize his passenger cars. There was opposition from Europe: three Type 30 Bugattis and three Mercedes driven by Christian Lautenschlager, Max Sailer and Christian Werner. Mercedes was virtually banned from racing in Europe except at the Targa Florio where, in 1922, it was the first company to race a supercharged car.

Millers took the first four places: Milton in one of the HCS Specials followed by Harry Hartz, Murphy and Hearne. Mercedes did not do well: Lautenschlager crashed, Sailer finished eighth and Werner 11th. Hearne took his 122 on to win the American National Championship in 1923. The Bugattis and Mercedes were the last European cars to enter Indianapolis for many years; in 1924, all the entries were American.

If Duesenberg had been out of the limelight in the 1923 Indianapolis, it came back with a vengeance in 1924. Two of the four cars were fitted with superchargers. The drivers were L. L. Corum

and Boyer. Boyer came from behind to lead by the second lap, but his supercharger broke a gear and he had to retire. Corum was lying in fifth place and, when he came in after 109 laps, Fred Duesenberg replaced him with Boyer with the words: 'Put that ship out in front or burn it up.'

It was an exciting finish. Boyer again came from behind, taking on Earl Cooper in a Studebaker and Murphy in his Miller to win by a narrow margin. Cooper was second and Murphy third. Superchargers were clearly the route to winning.

In 1925, Miller supercharged the 122 engine and sold conversion kits to previous customers. He also produced a front-wheel drive version. Duesenberg won Indianapolis that year with its supercharged car driven by Peter de Paolo, who took the average speed for the race above the 100 mph mark for the first time, at 101.127 mph. It was the high point of Fred Duesenberg's racing career. The next year, the formula changed again, down to 1.5 litres. Although Miller and Duesenberg both produced new cars, Miller gradually pulled ahead by producing them in numbers to sell to drivers. A rear-wheel drive car cost around $10,000, a front-wheel drive one $15,000. But for a good driver it was a sound investment. In 1925, the year de Paolo won the Indianapolis 500 and the American National Championship, he earned some $90,000.

The post-war years up to 1925 had seen enormous developments in racing cars and engines in America, and the birth of the single-seater. That progress was due to Duesenberg and Miller. The automobile industry in general did not put much effort into the sport, leaving it to the specialists. Duesenberg gradually withdrew from racing and for the rest of the decade Millers dominated American racing – the National Championships, record attempts, and Indianapolis where they won three out of five 500-mile events with Frank Lockhart in 1926, Louis Meyer in 1928 and Billy Arnold in 1930. Duesenberg won in 1927 and Simplex in 1929.

In Europe, over the same period, developments were no less exciting. A major innovation, in 1921, was the internationalization of Grand Prix racing. Before the war, the French Grand Prix had been *the* Grand Prix; other national events were known by local names. In September 1921, a week-long festival of motor racing was held at Brescia in northern Italy; the first race was the Italian Grand Prix. There were six starters: three 3-litre Ballots driven by de Palma, Chassagne and Goux, and three 8-cylinder Fiats driven by Wagner, Pietro Bordino and Ugo Sivocci. Bordino led for much of the race but he retired. The winner was Goux, giving Ballot its first Grand Prix win.

The Brescia week recognized another important trend in motor racing. The popularity of the Targa Florio among private entrants, mainly very rich men who could afford to buy cars and race for sport, had been obvious. But only manufacturers could enter the Grand Prix. The organizers therefore also staged a 'Gran Premio Gentlemen'. The winner was Count Giulio Masetti in his 1914 Grand Prix Mercedes; second was Tommaso Saccomani in a Ceirano. Third place went to a woman, Baroness Antonietta d'Avanso, in an Alfa Romeo.

ABOVE **Massed start:** the scene at the 1922 French Grand Prix at Duppigheim, near Strasbourg. It was the first major European event to abandon the practice of starting at timed intervals.

BELOW **Fewer finishers:** only three cars completed the 498-mile race, led by Felice Nazzaro in his flawed Fiat 804–404. Gordon Crosby's painting shows Nazzaro lapping Pierre de Vizcaya in a Bugatti Type 30 which came in second. Piero Marco was third in another Bugatti. Nazzaro's car was found to have a crack in the rear axle, similar to the fault which killed his nephew Biagio in the same race.

Races on closed public roads were exciting, but they were not profitable. To put racing on a sound financial footing, shorter circuits were specially built in most European countries during the 1920s. They differed from the American tracks in reflecting the road-racing tradition, although many included a banked oval as part of the course. One such was the Monza Autodrome, just outside Milan. It was built in 100 days from a standing start for the second Italian Grand Prix in 1922, and had 3.4 miles of road circuit and 2.8 miles of high-speed oval. One hundred thousand spectators came to see the first race for voiturettes when the gates opened on 3 September 1922. The event was hardly competitive: once Fiat announced it was running most manufacturers pulled out. But the result delighted the partisan crowd: Bordino, an ex-Fiat riding mechanic, driving a Fiat, won, followed by three more Fiats.

The 1922 French Grand Prix was held on 16 July on closed public roads near Strasbourg. Ettore Bugatti, who had regained his factory after the war, turned out a streamlined car shaped like a bullet with a tapering tail. The new Ballots were similar and Sunbeam entered a team with its new Henry-designed engine. But the strongest challengers were Fiat with a small, straightforward-looking car, the Tipo 804–404, with a 6-cylinder, double overhead camshaft engine giving 112 bhp at 5000 rpm. It was clearly the fastest in practice, reaching well over 100 mph down the straights. The 804 came from the design office of Guido Fornaca, who had been running Fiat's experimental department since 1906. Under his leadership, and with the backing of the company, it had become the training ground for the best racing engineers of the time.

Fiat's team of drivers was just as strong: the veteran Felice Nazzaro, his nephew Biagio Nazzaro in his first Grand Prix, and the very quick new man, Bordino. It was the first Grand Prix to

LEFT 'Chitty Chitty Bang Bang': the legendary racing car, the first of three to bear the name, was built by Count Louis Zborowski to race at Brooklands. He adapted a Mercedes chassis to take a 23-litre, 6-cylinder Maybach engine which had been used to power German Gotha bombers during the war. The car won its first race, the 'Short Handicap', on Easter Monday 1921.

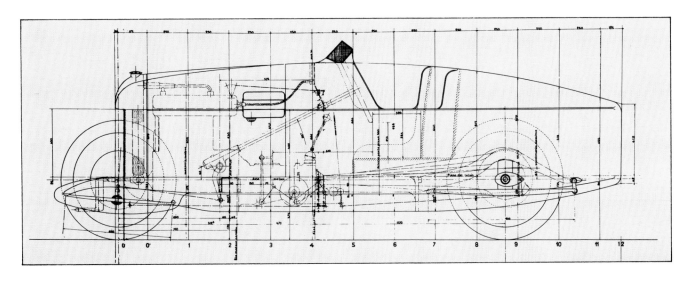

TOP Design: drawings of the Fiat 803–403 from Guido Fornaca's team of draughtsmen and engineers.

ABOVE Engineering: the 4-cylinder, supercharged Fiat 803–403 (No. 3) at the start of the Gran Premio delle Vetturette at Monza in 1923. Driven by Alessandro Cagno, it led from start to finish.

LEFT Art: Aldo Mazza's celebration of Fiat's period of supremacy which started in 1922.

use a massed start and the Fiats went into the lead immediately. Halfway through they were in first, second and third place and it looked like a landslide for the company. Then tragedy struck: Bordino's and Biagio Nazzaro's rear axles broke and they crashed, Biagio fatally. Felice Nazzaro, unaware of the accidents, drove on to win. Pierre de Vizcaya, second in a Bugatti, came in nearly an hour behind.

The enthusiasm of manufacturers to compete in the Italian Grand Prix at Monza two months later evaporated with the Fiat victory at Strasbourg. Pre-race entry had been huge with 39 cars, but on race day Mercedes, Benz, Sunbeam, Ballot and others did not turn up. There were only eight starters. These included three Fiats, their back axles strengthened, driven by Nazzaro, Bordino and Enrico Giaccone. De Vizcaya was there in a Bugatti. It was a Fiat triumph with Bordino first and Nazzaro second; de Vizcaya came third.

For the 1923 season, Fiat entered three of its new Tipo 805–405, a straight eight with a supercharger. The French Grand Prix was over a rough road circuit at Tours. The line-up was new and impressive: Sunbeam had poached one of Fiat's most talented designers, Vincent Bertarione, and their team included Guinness and Segrave. Its cars were virtual copies of the 1922 Fiat and not supercharged. Delage's engine was a V-12. Bugatti had another completely new shape.

Bordino took a commanding lead for Fiat, demonstrating the value of superchargers, and by the third lap only Guinness in the Sunbeam was anywhere near him. But the superchargers had been

LEFT Sensation: Italy salutes Carlo Salamano at the Monza Autodrome. His victory in the Italian Grand Prix of 1923 was a landmark for motor racing: the Fiat 805–405 was the first supercharged car to win a Grand Prix.

BELOW Innovation: the two 8-cylinder Fiat 805–405s driven by veteran Felice Nazzaro (8) and Salamano (14) charge past Ferdinando Minoia in the unsupercharged Benz (1). The Benz was innovative too: its engine was mounted between the driver and the back axle, a 'mid-engined' configuration 35 years ahead of its time.

mounted too low and ingested dust and stones which ruined the engines. All the Fiats dropped out leaving Segrave to win for Sunbeam, the first British driver to win a Grand Prix. It was the high point of Sunbeam's career in Continental road racing, but something of a hollow victory with the main opposition having dropped out.

Fiat modified its superchargers for the Italian Grand Prix at Monza on 9 September. The event saw one of the Miller's rare appearances in Europe. Murphy was looking to repeat his 1921 Grand Prix victory in a Miller 122, and Count Louis Zborowski was driving another; both were unsupercharged. Alfa Romeo, a little-known name at the time, entered the P.1 driven by Ascari. The French, including Bugatti, stayed away.

The result was a resounding victory for Fiat with Carlo Salamano winning from Nazzaro. It was the first major European race to be won by a supercharged car. Murphy was third: what the Millers had in power, they lacked in road holding and transmission quality for the road-racing type of circuit.

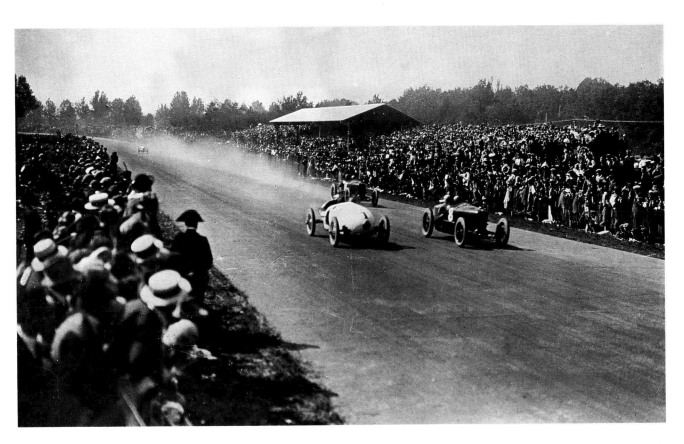

ALFA ROMEO: BIRTHPLACE OF LEGENDS

When Vittorio Jano moved from Fiat to Alfa Romeo in 1923, he brought a freshness and vitality to Alfa's design which was to have far-reaching consequences for the company and his own career. The P.2s set the standard for Grand Prix cars, and their string of wins in 1924 and 1925, and the first World Championship in 1925, gave them a sporting image on which the company was determined to capitalize.

The first road car was ready in 1925. The 6C, a 6-cylinder, 1500-cc, single overhead camshaft two-seater came on to the market just in time for a new road race run for the first time in 1927: the Mille Miglia, 1000 miles starting and finishing in Brescia, northern Italy. The event attracted the great Italian drivers of the day but was also open to amateurs. Seventy-seven cars started and 54 finished, the first of them 21 hours later; Alfas were seventh and ninth.

The following year, a works team headed by Giuseppe Campari and Giulio Ramponi entered and won; Alfas were also fourth, fifth and eighth. In 1929, a quarter of the entries were Alfas: they were available as the 1500-cc Turismo, the 1500-cc, double overhead camshaft Grand Turismo, and the double overhead camshaft and supercharged 1750-cc Super Sports. Campari drove a 2-litre version and won again for the works team. Achille Varzi was third in an Alfa and the cars also filled sixth to eighth places. In 1930, a relatively unknown ex-racing motor-cyclist, Tazio Nuvolari, made it three in a row for Alfa which also filled second, third, fourth, eighth, ninth and tenth places.

RIGHT Vittorio Jano was born in 1891 and began working in the motor industry at the age of 18. He started with Fiat in 1911, and remained one of the most imaginative designers in Italian motor racing until his death in 1965.

FAR RIGHT Enzo Ferrari persuaded Jano to move to Alfa Romeo. Born in 1895, Ferrari started by driving and came second in the Targa Florio in 1920 in an Alfa. But he was not a natural driver: in the 1924 French Grand Prix he was down to drive a P.2, but he suffered a nervous breakdown and withdrew. As team manager, he became one of the towering figures of the sport.

RIGHT In the 1924 French Grand Prix, Antonio Ascari in a P.2 led from lap 10, until he pulled into the pits on the last lap to change plugs. His engine was wrecked and despite the strenuous efforts of Ramponi, it refused to restart, leaving the race to his team-mate Campari.

RIGHT Antonio Ascari with his mechanic, Giulio Ramponi, at the Italian Grand Prix at Monza, 1924. Alfa P.2s driven by Ascari, Louis Wagner, Giuseppe Campari and Ferdinando Minoia, took the first four places.

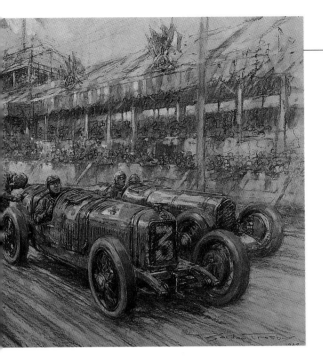

In 1924, superchargers were almost universal and the French Grand Prix saw the debut of two cars which would become legends. Enzo Ferrari, who was running the Alfa Romeo racing team, had managed to poach another of Fiat's star engineers, Vittorio Jano, who produced the supercharged Alfa Romeo P.2. It had already won its first race, the Circuit of Cremona, in June. Bugatti, though he steadfastly held out against supercharging, fielded a team of five exquisite Type 35s. They were more traditional than the previous two years' entries and beautifully designed and finished. Delage was getting 120 bhp from the V-12 engine. The Sunbeam team was also there. Fiat did not bring out a new car, but improved its previous models.

The driver line-up was also magnificent: Nazzaro, nearing the end of his racing career, and Bordino for Fiat; Campari, Wagner and the highly talented Ascari, who had won in the P.2 at Cremona, for Alfa Romeo; Albert Divo, Robert Benoist and the tireless Thomas for Delage. Sunbeam was back with Segrave and Guinness. The race marked another first: Zborowski had entered in a Miller, the first time a privately entered car had been accepted in the French Grand Prix.

It was a classic race. Segrave took the lead followed by Divo and Ascari. The Type 35 Bugattis all suffered tyre failures. While Segrave was in the pits Bordino went into the lead, chased by Ascari in the P.2. Ascari passed him, then Bordino won it back, then Campari came through the field. Bordino's brakes failed. Ascari took the lead followed by team-mate Campari, then his engine gave up, leaving Campari to win for Alfa from Divo and Benoist for Delage, followed by Wagner for Alfa.

The Italian Grand Prix which followed on 19 October at Monza was something of an anti-climax. Fiat announced its withdrawal from racing – fed up with losing the talent it trained to others, who then beat them – and the French stayed away. There were only 12 entries, the strongest from Alfa and Mercedes. There was tragedy when Zborowski, one of the great 'gentleman' racers, was killed driving for Mercedes, but triumph for Alfa as Ascari, Wagner, Campari and Ferdinando Minoia came in first, second, third and fourth.

'LE PUR-SANG DES AUTOMOBILES'

Ettore Bugatti's cars, like the horses he loved, were thoroughbreds. Bugatti was born into an artistic family in Milan in 1881, but moved to France early in his career. Like Harry Miller in America, he was an intuitive rather than a trained engineer: if it looked right and felt right, it was right.

He was also stubborn, autocratic, vain and deeply conservative, especially when it came to adopting new ideas which were not his own. A famous quote attributed to him after criticism of his brakes was: 'I build my cars to go, not stop.'

In the dark days of Grand Prix racing in the late 1920s, he produced the Type 35B with a 2.3-litre supercharged engine. The car dominated such Grand Prix racing as there was, in the hands of drivers like William Grover Williams and Louis Chiron.

Bugatti was finally reconciled to double overhead camshaft, supercharged engines by his son, Jean, and, indirectly, by Miller. In 1929, the American Leon Duray brought a pair of Millers to Europe but exchanged them for three Type 43 Bugattis. Miller had used double overhead camshafts and superchargers for many years. Bugatti copied the Miller engines to produce the Type 51, which was to the early 1930s what the Type 35 had been to the late 1920s.

RIGHT **Ettore Bugatti was always 'Le Patron'. He treated his employees, including his drivers, like members of a vast family with him at its head; great dinners were held at his Molsheim home when his cars won. He was a man of ideas who surrounded himself with others who could carry them out. He died in 1947.**

LEFT ABOVE **Works driver Bartolomeo Constantini, on his way to his second successive Targa Florio victory for Bugatti in 1926.**

LEFT **Racing behind the wheel of a Type 35 Bugatti – an amateur driver's dream.**

The following year, 1925, saw the climax of this extraordinary period of technical advance and expansion in motor racing. Europe followed America in abandoning riding mechanics. A long road circuit at Spa-Francorchamps was prepared for the first Belgian Grand Prix. In France, the sport finally succumbed to the move towards specially built tracks with an artificial road circuit and high-speed oval at Montlhéry, south of Paris. A second such track was planned for Miramas, near Marseilles, for 1926.

In 1925, the first World Championship was organized, taking in the French, Italian and Belgian Grands Prix and the Indianapolis 500. The contest was between manufacturers, not drivers: Grand Prix racing was still the province of the motor industry rather than its participants.

Four teams were at Spa on 28 June for the Belgian Grand Prix – Alfa Romeo, Delage, Bugatti and Sunbeam – but they could muster only seven cars between them. Delage had supercharged its V-12 engine, which now produced 180 bhp – 90 bhp/litre – but it was very complex. The Alfa P.2s were still clearly on top and gradually the Delage, Sunbeam and Bugatti drivers retired, leaving Ascari and Campari circling alone. Ascari was well in the lead. The crowd, which included substantial numbers of French spectators, showed its displeasure by hissing the red cars. Jano, to emphasize the Alfas' superiority, responded by having a table and chair brought to the front of the Alfa Romeo pits where he enjoyed a full lunch while his drivers stormed to victory.

There were 14 entries for the French Grand Prix at Montlhéry on 26 July. Ascari went into his customary lead early on and the Bugattis were left well behind the supercharged cars. Devoid of serious competition from the other teams, a battle developed between Ascari and Campari in their Alfa P.2s. Ascari clipped a fence and his car turned over several times: he was injured and died on the way to hospital. The Alfas were withdrawn as a mark of respect, resulting in a first and second for Delage. It was another hollow victory, but it was the first time a French manufacturer had won the French Grand Prix since Peugeot in 1913.

PREVIOUS PAGES, ABOVE AND RIGHT Designer Grand Prix car: the Type 35 Bugatti which started its long racing career in 1924. Many still appear in historic events.

The French driver René Dreyfus started as an amateur and won his first major race in a Type 35 Bugatti: 'You could place the car wherever you wanted, the road holding was fantastic ... the precision of the steering was something fantastic.'

Ivan Dutton says of his Bugatti: 'It's got the most fabulous gearbox ... it goes from first to second as fast as you can move the lever. Normally you have to count three in vintage cars.'

Delage stayed away from the Italian Grand Prix on 6 September, fearful of taking on the mighty Alfas on their home ground. Duesenberg, fresh from its second triumph at Indianapolis, and spurred on by hopes of winning the World Championship, entered Milton and Peter Kreis. Duesenbergs were more suited to European conditions than the Millers but they were unable to beat the Alfas. Gastone Brilli-Peri won, followed by Campari. Bartholomew Constantini was third in a Bugatti and Milton fourth. It was the last time a major American entry crossed the Atlantic for many years.

The year ended with Alfa Romeo the first World Champion; Duesenberg came second and Bugatti third. Alfa incorporated a laurel wreath into its badge to mark the triumph.

It was the high point of Grands Prix for some time. In 1926, engine size was reduced to 1.5 litres. The manufacturers, contemplating the cost of producing new engines and new cars each year, with few tangible rewards, declined to put up the investment. Both Alfa Romeo and Sunbeam pulled out. With Fiat already gone, Grand Prix racing was left to the French pair, Delage and Bugatti. Only three cars, all Bugattis, turned up for the 1926 French Grand Prix at Miramas. They raced, but only Goux finished and, inevitably, won. He then retired.

The first British Grand Prix was held in 1926 at Brooklands, on a course modified with sandbanks to provide road-racing conditions. A Delage, driven first by René Sénéchal and then by Wagner, won. Malcolm Campbell was second in a Bugatti, followed by Benoist in another Delage. In 1927, Benoist, again driving for Delage, won all four European races, and the title, in the World Championship.

Lacking the excitement of competition in the earlier years, from 1928 Grand Prix racing went into a decline. The focus shifted to Formula Libre events such as the Targa Florio, and other lesser-known races, in which a high proportion of drivers owned their cars and competed on their own account. In 1925, Constantini had won the Targa for Bugatti in a Type 35; he returned the following year and won it again. The Type 35 was produced with a 2.3-litre unsupercharged engine under the designation Type 35T, the 'T' was for Targa, for people who wanted to take part in the race. In 1927, Constantini was back at the Targa, this time managing the works team and looking after the increasing number of amateurs who were entering too. Many were amateurs only in the sense that they did not rely on driving for a living; they were 'gentlemen professionals', men (and a tiny number of women) who enjoyed the racing lifestyle and were talented and rich enough to support their indulgence. With and for such people, Bugatti made the Targa Florio virtually its own, winning the event in 1927, 1928 and 1929, but also enabling many drivers to take part by selling them the cars to do so.

UNSUNG HEROES

LEFT **Sharing the workload: mechanic Giulio Ramponi helps Antonio Ascari to push their P.2 in the 1924 Spanish Grand Prix.**

ABOVE **Sharing the dangers: in the same race, Kenelm Lee Guinness's Sunbeam after the crash in which his mechanic, Jack Barrott, was killed.**

For the first 30 years of racing, riding mechanics were both necessary and obligatory. But as engines became more and more reliable, and races shorter on the specially built tracks, it became increasingly clear that their proper place was in the pits rather than in the car. In the early days, they also had a social role, serving the driver in much the same way as a groom served a horseman. Many mechanics became drivers; in 1925, one of the main arguments against dispensing with them was that there would be nowhere for drivers to learn their trade. On long-distance races, such as the Mille Miglia a second person was still necessary but they were co-drivers rather than mechanics.

BELOW **Helping on the corners: Henri Fournier's mechanic leans out to balance the car as it goes into a corner on the Paris–Berlin race of 1901.**

FAR LEFT **Learning on the job: Attilio Marinoni with Giuseppe Campari after winning the French Grand Prix in 1924. Marinoni drove for Alfa in the 1930s.**

BROOKLANDS' HEYDAYS

Brooklands was the first purpose-built motor-racing track in the world, constructed to encourage the development of the motor car and racing in Britain. It lasted from 1907 to 1939 and provided a great deal of enjoyment for a great many people. However, it did little to further Britain's position internationally: cars which succeeded there rarely succeeded anywhere else.

The reason was that racing at Brooklands, like Royal Ascot, the Henley Regatta and Wimbledon, was as much a social as a sporting event. In the early days, it was seen as being very similar to horse racing, a sport with which many of the Brooklands committee, including the Duke of Westminster, Prince Francis of Teck, Lord Montagu and Sir Redvers Buller, were familiar. Race days were 'meetings' and bookmakers took bets. Numbers were not permitted on cars; instead, drivers had to wear 'colours' like jockeys. Cars were 'handicapped', originally by price, later on by performance. Rule Four of the regulations stated that, 'motor cars must be shod with india-rubber tyres'.

Brooklands was a club run by a particular social group for its own pleasure; the technical advance of motor cars was not its their primary concern. It was also the only place in Britain where races were run. Entrance to the public enclosures was expensive, ensuring that the sport was beyond the pockets of most working people.

The cars were fast but the racing, compared with European events, was unexciting. By the 1920s, when new tracks on the Continent were being built with both banking and road circuits, Brooklands was obsolete.

Speed record attempts were a feature of Brooklands, and two holders of the World Speed Record – Henry Segrave and Malcolm Campbell – both knighted for their achievements, began there.

The cult of the gentleman professional found its most eloquent expression in the 24-hour race at Le Mans, where a small group of rich young men, most of them English, made a name for themselves as 'The Bentley Boys'. The British car maker Walter Owen Bentley built a range of heavy, powerful, well-engineered cars – once described by Bugatti as 'the fastest lorries in the world'.

They were ideal for the 24-hour Grand Prix d'Endurance at Le Mans, which had first been held in 1923 as the ultimate test of the stamina of touring cars. For such a marathon, two drivers were needed. Bentley was not interested at first but, in 1924, a Bentley owner, John Duff, entered privately in his 3-litre car, with Frank Clement, and won against 39 French cars. In 1925 and 1926, Bentley entered a team without success. But he learnt a great deal about the race and attracted around him the group of playboys who wanted to win the event. In 1927, that combination led to a Bentley victory by Dudley Benjafield and Sammy Davis. Britain sorely lacked motor-racing victories, particularly on the Continent, and to mark the occasion _The Autocar_ held a dinner at the Savoy hotel at which the winning car was guest of honour.

In 1928, Bentley won again with Woolf Barnato, who was partly financing Bentley to build the cars, and Bernard Rubin driving a 4.5-litre model. Five Bentleys were entered for the 1929 Le Mans and four of them finished first, second, third and fourth, crossing the line together.

Nothing was too good for The Bentley Boys. They gave the British public something to cheer about: British cars, in British racing green, with British drivers, beating foreign competition on its own ground. In 1930, Barnato won once again, with Glen Kidston, making it four Bentley victories in a row.

It was too good to last. Bentley was in financial trouble brought about, directly or indirectly, by the sheer cost of racing and the company's concentration on the sport. The Wall Street crash in

LEFT Some horse-racing expressions such as 'paddock' survive to the present day.

ABOVE FAR LEFT 'Taking the cement' was the expression club members used for racing. This 'Dutch Clog' Austin was built by Sir Herbert Austin for Brooklands in 1931.

ABOVE LEFT 'The right crowd and no crowding' was the motto of the track; entrance for the Grand Prix was 5s a head and £1 for entry to the paddock.

OVERLEAF One of the 4.5-litre Lorraine Dietrichs in the pits during the 24-hour race at Le Mans in 1926, the year they came first, second and third.

1929 had its effect on the fortunes of some of his customers and the money began to dry up. There was no works team at Le Mans in 1931 and although Bentleys were entered privately, they were not successful. What remained of the company was taken over by Rolls-Royce.

Nobody could buy the legends which men like Bentley, Bugatti, Miller, Jano, Fornaca, Delage, Ballot, Henry and Duesenberg had created. Many of their cars are preserved, and still raced, today by people who cherish them and the spirit of that age. It was a golden period for designers, drivers – whether gentlemen or professionals – and spectators alike.

The technical improvements brought about by the sport were gradually incorporated into cars for domestic consumers, but the process was slow. Mass manufacturers were generally not inclined to support racing, leaving it to the dedicated band of specialists.

During the 1920s, the racing traditions of Europe and America had grown steadily wider apart. From 1930, into the Depression, they had very little in common. In that year, the American formula was changed to one based on 'stock' car engines, variations of those the public were able to buy in showrooms, and riding mechanics were brought back.

It was the end of an era. The board speedways, or 'roaring boards', had gradually succumbed to rot and to the increasing cost of keeping them safe. The world in which Miller, the architect of the most stimulating period in American racing history, had flourished and entertained, disappeared in the new economic climate and with the changing needs of the automobile industry. Specialist car makers like Miller, artisans as opposed to producers, had no place in the new scheme of things. Miller, who put most of the money he made back into his beloved engines and cars, appealed to only a very small market. In October 1931 he made formal arrangements with his creditors. He was failing to meet his payroll and Offenhauser was taking promissory notes on various items of equipment in lieu of pay. In 1933, Miller filed for bankruptcy and his house and ranch were sold over his head.

THE BENTLEY BOYS

The atmosphere in the Bentley camp at Le Mans was like that of a fighter squadron in war: a small, dedicated group following a dangerous pursuit and enjoying the life that went with it. The drivers were hand-picked by Walter Owen Bentley, who cultivated a strong team spirit, and they had to submerge their individual aspirations to the needs of the team. Many of them started their racing careers at Brooklands.

Bentley was attracted to Le Mans because it was a perfect forum in which to show the quality of his cars; the prominence they gained from racing and winning made them particularly popular in France.

BELOW **Walter Owen Bentley about to drive one of his cars in the 1922 Tourist Trophy, Britain's only road race, on the Isle of Man. It was the first TT since 1914: Jean Chassagne** won for Sunbeam with Frank Clement second in a Bentley. O. Payne was third in a Vauxhall, Bentley fourth and Douglas Hawks, also in a Bentley, fifth.

LEFT AND BOTTOM The 1930 4.5-litre 'Blower' Bentley. To qualify for running at Le Mans, 50 production cars had to be built; 40 of the original run have survived. The prominent Amherst-Villiers supercharger increased power to 175 bhp at 3500 rpm giving a speed of 105 mph. Racing versions were boosted to 240 bhp at 4900 rpm.

ABOVE The Bentley Boys at Le Mans in 1929, the year of their great one, two, three, four victory. Tim Birkin (third from right) was part of the winning duo with Woolf Barnato, the company chairman; Jack Dunfee (front, left) was second with Glen Kidston.

— CHAPTER FOUR —
RARE BREEDS

During the early 1930s, the heroes and the excitement of motor racing provided a source of escape from the miseries of the Depression. The sport grew: partly because it was entertaining, but it was also due to the relaxation of regulations, particularly at the topmost level where the strict formulae based on engine size and weight, which had governed Grand Prix racing since 1914, had been effectively abandoned since 1928. The national Grands Prix were still run, but in addition there were local races, run under Formula Libre conditions, which took the name of the place where they were held. These gave rise to events such as the Marne, Montenero and the Rome Grands Prix.

The cost of racing was too much for major manufacturers who were also producers of domestic cars and they pulled out, leaving the field to a wonderfully colourful band of drivers who raced as privateers, in partnerships or in teams. They bought their cars from specialist racing-car builders such as Bugatti, Alfa Romeo and Maserati. These companies, particularly Bugatti, signed up the top drivers and entered their own works teams, but their business was to supply the needs of the great mass of independent drivers who raced in Formula Libre events. Motor racing flourished in this deregulated form and at the top, a few names, the most talented men, became stars.

In the late 1920s, this market was dominated by Bugatti and one of the most accomplished '*bugattistes*' was from Monaco, Louis Chiron: in 1928, he won the European, Rome and Marne

LEFT **Europe's successful first pure-bred single-seater: the Alfa Romeo Type B.**

Grands Prix for Bugatti, and repeated the hat trick in 1929, adding the San Sebastian and German Grands Prix for good measure. In the same year, a private entrant, Grover Williams, won the first Monaco Grand Prix in a Bugatti with E. Bouriano second in another.

But Bugatti's position was frequently challenged by Alfa Romeo. The change in the formula, which followed Alfa's World Championship triumph in 1925, prompted them to sell the P.2 Grand Prix cars and they enjoyed an extended career in the hands of private entrants, among them Giuseppe Campari and Count Gastone Brilli-Peri. Before the start of the European Grand Prix at Monza in 1928, Campari sold his P.2 to a young, taciturn driver, Achille Varzi, and then shared the driving with him to come second behind Chiron's Bugatti. Varzi then went on to win the 1929 Monza, Rome and Montenero Grands Prix, and the Bordino Prize, in the P.2.

In 1930, Alfa Romeo bought the P.2s back from the private entrants and handed them over to a new organization called Scuderia Ferrari. Enzo Ferrari had persevered as a driver, but he was in greater demand at Alfa Romeo as a 'fixer' and organizer. Scuderia was his team, which he effectively ran as Alfa Romeo's racing department. He hired the top drivers to race for him and supported Alfa's other clients, the private entrants, with technical back-up at the races.

One event which flourished spectacularly during this period was the Mille Miglia, founded in 1927. In 1929, there had been 72 starters but in 1930, when the organizers, the Auto Club di Brescia, introduced a Utility class, limited by engine size and price to make sure the entries represented the kind of car which could be bought in the showroom, the entry list nearly doubled and there were 135 starters.

Campari had won the 1928 and 1929 Mille Miglia for the Alfa Romeo works team in a specially prepared version of the 6C sports car. In 1930, he was joined by two rising stars of Italian racing, Tazio Nuvolari and Varzi, who were also the bitterest of personal rivals. Maserati and Fiat also entered teams in what had already become a classic. The only foreign entry came from Mercedes who sent a single car, a SSK sports, driven by its own rising star, Rudolf Caracciola. He was there mainly to gain experience of the race.

The principality of Monaco has had a long association with motor sport through two events: the Monte Carlo Rally (BELOW), first run in 1911, and the Monaco Grand Prix (RIGHT), which started in 1929. Both were dreamed up by the energetic president of the Automobile Club of Monaco, Anthony Noghes, and both have survived to the present day as premier events in their field.

From Brescia, the 1930 Mille Miglia criss-crossed northern Italy for its 1000 miles – 16 hours driving for the professionals, and over 24 hours for the amateurs. Each car had two drivers but Nuvolari and Varzi rarely shared the wheel with their co-drivers – each wanted to win. The slower Utility cars left first, at one-minute intervals. The number on the side of the cars indicated the time they had left Brescia, giving spectators along the route an idea of where they were placed.

Once the professionals were off, Luigi Arcangeli went into the lead in a Maserati followed by Nuvolari, with Varzi and Caracciola fighting for third place. Arcangeli crashed, putting Nuvolari in the lead followed by Varzi, Caracciola and Campari: by the time they reached Rome, the race had become a duel between Varzi and Nuvolari. Varzi was ahead in the field, but Nuvolari was ahead on time as they set out over the mountainous backbone of Italy. During the night, thousands of people turned out along the route with torches to show the drivers the way.

When the leaders reached Bologna, Varzi was 3 minutes ahead on the road, but Nuvolari was 7 minutes ahead on time. As dawn broke, Nuvolari had made up the 3 minutes and saw Varzi's car ahead. He put out his lights and crept up on his great rival unobserved, then flashed them on again as he went past. Nuvolari was 20 minutes ahead by the time he crossed the line to win, with Varzi second and Campari third. It was a hat trick for Alfa, who also won the 1.5-litre class.

Nuvolari and Varzi met again three weeks later at Italy's other sports car race, the Targa Florio. The previous five races had been won by Bugattis and the Italian crowd was looking to Alfa Romeo, Varzi and Nuvolari to capture the Targa Florio for Italy. Ferrari had modified the P.2 engines, increasing the power output to 175 bhp which gave them a top speed of 140 mph. The cars were to be driven by Varzi and Campari, but Ferrari decided that they were too dangerous for the mountain circuit. Varzi protested: Nuvolari was driving a 6C Alfa and Varzi wanted any advantage he could get to beat him. After a heated argument, Ferrari relented and Varzi got his way.

THE MILLE MIGLIA

Italy's great road race was designed as a way of popularizing motor cars at a time when they were a rarity on most Italian roads; it was also a means of improving car design and reliability. It succeeded in both aims: 1000 miles of rugged racing was one of the severest tests of a car's reliability. Driving in the race became a symbol of virility, a rite of passage almost, for some young Italian drivers.

Cars started from Brescia at one-minute intervals, Numbers painted on the side indicated the time they had started, giving spectators an idea of how they were placed.

ABOVE **Mille Miglia Alfa:** one of the privately entered 1.5-litre, 6-cylinder sports cars in the 1930 race.

RIGHT **Mille Miglia Fiats:** the 514 Spider (in front) which won the 1930 race and the Balilla Coppa D'oro (behind) which won the 1100-cc class in 1934, inside the Lingotto, Fiat's factory in Turin.

BELOW The Lingotto's rooftop test track.

The Bugatti works team of four included
Chiron, Albert Divo, Williams and Count Conelli.
Maserati also entered a team of its new 175-bhp 8C-
2500 cars driven by Arcangeli, Ernesto Maserati,
Umberto Borzacchini and Luigi Fagioli. Varzi
stormed through the Bugattis into the lead, breaking the lap record on the first lap; Nuvolari did not
have the power to catch him. Divo crashed, leaving
Chiron the only Bugatti driver with any hope of
catching Varzi. As a result of the pounding of the
mountain roads Varzi's spare wheel worked its
mounting loose, which in turn punctured the fuel
tank. It could not be repaired so Varzi had to stop
to refuel more often. Chiron, in a momentary lapse
of concentration, crashed into a wall damaging a
front wheel. He and his mechanic replaced it but
they slipped a little further behind.

Riding mechanics were still carried in the Targa
Florio. On the last lap, Varzi's mechanic took a
spare can of fuel with him in case they ran out and,
on a downhill stretch, he leaned over the back and
tried to pour petrol into the tank while they were

ABOVE The master: Tazio Nuvolari in 1931.

RIGHT Cockpit of the Alfa Romeo Type B, Monoposto.

BELOW The start of the epic duel between Achille Varzi and
Nuvolari in the 1933 Monte Carlo Grand Prix. Varzi's Type 51
Bugatti (No. 10) is just ahead of Umberto Borzacchini's Alfa
Monza (No. 26) which finished second after Nuvolari's Alfa
(No. 28, far left) broke down on the last lap.

ABOVE AND RIGHT **English Racing Automobiles:** Britain's single-seater, the 1.5-litre Type B ERA voiturette. The 6-cylinder engine was supercharged, giving up to 160 bhp.

moving. He spilt some on the exhaust and the fuel caught fire. They were only just ahead of Chiron and a stop could cost them the race: Varzi drove on while his mechanic tried to beat out the flames with his cushion. They won, giving the P.2 a last glorious moment by capturing the Targa Florio for Italy. The crowd was ecstatic: Bugatti's dominance of the Sicilian classic was ended in style.

Italian road racing was in Italian hands, but on the Grand Prix circuit, Bugatti and Maserati were still sharing the honours. Chiron won the 1930 Monaco and Belgian Grands Prix, René Dreyfus the Marne, and Philippe Etancelin the French Grand Prix for Bugatti. Varzi, now driving for Maserati, won the Spanish and the Monza Grands Prix; Arcangeli won at Rome in a Maserati.

To stay competitive, Bugatti and Alfa Romeo both introduced new cars for the 1931 season. Bugatti brought out the Type 51. It had similar lines to the Type 35 but the engine, based on the Miller, was new: 2.3 litres and supercharged. Chiron won at Monaco and Varzi, back with Bugatti, at Tunis, both in Type 51s. Grands Prix were now run over 10 hours, requiring two drivers, and Chiron and Varzi shared a Type 51 for the French and Belgian events, winning both races.

Alfa Romeo replied with two new cars from Vittorio Jano: a 2.3-litre sports car, the Monza, which could be used for Grands Prix, and a Grand-Prix car, the 12-cylinder Type A. Nuvolari took the Monza to Sicily for the Targa Florio, where Varzi was driving a Bugatti Type 51. The scene was set for another great match between the two men: the Bugatti was more powerful, giving Varzi his customary early lead and a new lap record, but the Alfas managed to stay with him even if they could not beat him. For most of the race Varzi looked uncatchable, then the weather broke and the roads were soon running with rain-water. The Bugatti had no mudguards and Varzi was sprayed with a fine mud. Although the Alfa drivers were not in much better shape, they were protected by mudguards so the bad weather gave them an advantage. Nuvolari took it, winning by 5 minutes from Borzacchini and 7 minutes from Varzi.

At the Italian Grand Prix two weeks later, Nuvolari and Arcangeli were to drive the Type A

Alfas. It was a heavy, unwieldy car with two 6-cylinder engines mounted in parallel. Arcangeli was killed in practice and Jano was tempted to withdraw the cars. Then politics intervened in the form of a telegram from the Italian dictator, Benito Mussolini: Alfa was to compete and win for the honour of Italy. But Nuvolari's car broke down and he had to share Campari's Monza. Varzi and Chiron were again sharing a Type 51, but they retired. Nuvolari and Campari won, followed by Borzacchini and Ferdinando Minoia for Alfa.

BELOW The man behind the ERA: the elegant Raymond Mays (standing) was one of Britain's leading racing drivers in the 1930s, but he wanted to drive a British car and in 1934 started building cars next to his home in Lincolnshire. Earl Howe (in car) at 53, is about to practise for the 1937 Junior Car Club's 200-mile race at Donington in his ERA.

RIGHT A total of 19 ERAs were built between 1934 and 1939. They were driven by private entrants, mainly in Britain, and had only moderate success against foreign opposition. They continued to be raced long after the Second World War and most still appear at historic events.

Alfa Romeo was beginning to shake Bugatti's grip on Grand-Prix racing. The brutish Type A had not been a success, but the Monza on the other hand, even though underpowered for Grands Prix, had triumphed. Jano wanted to build a lighter car with better handling qualities for these events and the Alfa Romeo management gave him the go-ahead for the 1932 season. He designed a slim single-seater with two drive shafts, one to each rear wheel, which enabled the driver to be positioned lower in the car and improved weight distribution. Jano would have liked a completely new engine, but there was not enough money so he took the 2.3-litre Monza engine, increased its capacity to 2.6 litres and fitted two superchargers giving it 215 bhp. The result was the Type B, also known as the Mono-posto (literally 'single-seater') or P.3. The P.3s were run as a works team by Alfa Romeo, while the Monzas were handed over to Scuderia Ferrari.

What the P.3 could not out-run on the straights, it could out-perform on the corners, especially in the hands of an expert. Alfa had two of the sport's most talented drivers in their works team: Nuvolari and Caracciola. Caracciola had won the 1931 Mille Miglia for Mercedes, but the Germans had pulled out of racing because of the cost. Caracciola wanted to go on competing so joined Alfa.

Nuvolari drove the P.3 to its first victory in the 1932 Italian Grand Prix, then to another in the French event. Caracciola won the German and Monza Grands Prix. Nuvolari won the Targa Florio again and Alfa took the first seven places in the Mille Miglia. They were back on top, despite everything that Bugatti and Maserati could throw at them. But success on that scale came at a price: in 1933, the company was in such poor shape financially that racing had to be stopped. Alfa pulled out but kept the P.3s in storage. Despite the poor economic climate, the number of Grands Prix continued to grow, but in 1933 Bugatti was the only company to field a works team. Nuvolari and Borzacchini moved to Scuderia Ferrari.

ROAD RACING COMES TO BRITAIN

In 1931 Fred Craner of the Derby & District Motor Club was given permission to build a motor-cycle racing circuit through the woods of Donington Park. The races were so popular that, in 1933, he widened the track to make Britain's first road-racing circuit for cars.

In 1935, Craner organized the Donington Grand Prix. Most of the drivers were British, in a mixture of continental and British cars. It was won by Richard Shuttleworth in an Alfa Romeo P.3 Monoposto. The Donington Grand Prix of 1936 attracted a bigger field, many of them from the Continent, and was won by Hans Ruesch and Richard Seaman in another Alfa. In

1937, the event was granted full international status and the regular fans were treated to full teams from Mercedes and Auto Union then at their peak. It was Donington's heyday, but it was short-lived: the 1938 event was run at the time of the Munich Crisis and the following year there was no race because of the war.

Donington was taken over by the War Office as a vehicle depot. When they gave it up in 1956, it was still littered with thousands of useless vehicles. It was bought by a local man, Tom Wheatcroft, who steadily restored the track and built up the world's biggest collection of historic Grand Prix cars in the museum.

ABOVE Tazio Nuvolari driving the Auto Union Type D in the 1938 Donington Grand Prix which he won at the ripe old age of 46.

LEFT Richard Seaman, a talented British driver who was signed by Mercedes, taking Coppice Corner on his way to third place behind Lang and Nuvolari in the 1938 Donington Grand Prix.

FAR LEFT The Grands Prix were the highpoints of the season, but Donington was the venue for other races which gave British fans a taste for the excitement of road racing.

TOP Grand Prix 1937: the cream of German drivers and cars sweep past the lone British ERA driven by Charles Martin. Hermann Lang (2) is leading for Mercedes followed by Caracciola (1), von Brauchitsch (3), Richard Seaman (4), Bernd Rosemeyer (5) for Auto Union (who won the race), then Otto Müller (7) and Rudi Hasse (6).

The Monaco Grand Prix opened the 1933 season with an innovation: it was the first race in Europe in which starting positions were allocated according to performance in practice. Nuvolari and Caracciola both crashed in practice. Nuvolari damaged only his car, but Caracciola was severely injured. Varzi put up the fastest time in practice in his Bugatti, and started from the best position on the front row of the grid. He led from the start, but was soon under pressure from his old adversary, Nuvolari, in an Alfa Monza. The race became a personal battle between the two men. The lead swapped back and forth for the rest of the 100 laps, with Nuvolari leading more often than Varzi. On the last lap, Nuvolari was ahead and looked set for victory, but Varzi managed to pass him, only to be overtaken moments later. With only a short distance to go, there was little to lose if the cars blew up, so both drivers pushed their engines well beyond normal operating limits. The Alfa gave up first, bursting an oil pipe. In possibly the greatest duel between the two, Varzi was the winner. Ever competitive, Nuvolari tried vainly to push his stricken car over the line for a place.

They met again at the Belgian Grand Prix where Nuvolari, driving a Maserati, avenged himself by beating Varzi in his Type 51. Nuvolari left Scuderia Ferrari to drive for Maserati, while Chiron and Fagioli joined the team just as Ferrari managed to talk Alfa Romeo into releasing the P.3s. At the Italian Grand Prix, always the great battleground for the Italian cars and drivers, Chiron, Fagioli and Piero Taruffi drove the P.3s. The main opposition came from Nuvolari and Goffredo Zehender for Maserati. Nuvolari managed to hold off all challenges from the Scuderia team's Alfas until, with a 30-second lead over Fagioli, a burst tyre cost him the race. Fagioli won, putting the P.3 back on top where it stayed for the rest of the season.

The Monza Grand Prix was held the same day. Campari announced that he was to retire after the race and pursue a career in opera singing. During a heat, oil was spilled on the South Curve and not properly cleaned up. Campari and Borzacchini came into the curve together in a later heat, skidded on the oil, crashed and both were killed.

Speeds had been rising to around 140–150 mph, mainly as a result of bigger engines and the use of superchargers. The Association Internationale des Automobile Clubs Reconnus (AIACR), the international governing body of the sport, was concerned at this trend and for the 1934, 1935 and 1936 seasons, it decreed a weight limit of 750 kg without driver, fuel or oil. There was no restriction on engine size, but the AIACR hoped that the weight limit would force designers to use lighter and therefore smaller, less powerful, engines which would in turn restrict speed. But it had not taken into account the ingenuity of designers. The change in formula, coming at the moment it did, had precisely the opposite effect.

The new formula was announced just as Adolf Hitler came to power in Germany. He was a motor-racing enthusiast, and he also saw the possibility of using German engineering excellence to produce racing cars which would beat all comers and, in so doing, provide propaganda for his vision of Germany. He wanted German drivers and cars to be ambassadors for the Reich, and proposed a subsidy of 450,000 marks a year (around £45,000) to be made available to any company who would take up the challenge.

Mercedes, who had been out of racing for two years, applied, and there was a second application from a consortium of four German companies – Audi, DKW, Wanderer and Horch – all of whom had suffered during the Depression and who had clubbed together to form Auto Union. The money was split between the two concerns, bonuses were added for coming first, second and third, and special tax arrangements were agreed for other investment made by the companies in supporting their racing. The injection of new money prompted Mercedes and Auto Union to build completely new cars. Alfa Romeo, Maserati and Bugatti lacked the finance to do the same; instead they had to adapt their existing cars to the new formula.

Auto Union brought in the independent car designer Dr Ferdinand Porsche. He had been chief engineer at Mercedes in the 1920s, but had set up his own design bureau in Berlin. By November 1933, the Auto Union Type A was ready for testing. Revolutionary in concept and appearance, it instantly made all other Grand-Prix cars of the period seem obsolete. It was streamlined with the engine mounted in the 'mid-engined' position, between the driver and the rear axle. The advantage of this position was that the engine and gearbox and final drive were all in one compact unit, cutting down on power losses. In addition, with the drive shaft no longer going through the cockpit, the driver could be seated lower down. The Type A

had independent suspension for each wheel and a supercharged V-16, 4.4-litre engine which produced 295 bhp.

Hitler inspected the new Mercedes W25 at the company headquarters in Stuttgart early in 1934. Mercedes' chief designer, Dr Hans Nibel, had come up with a more conventional layout than the Auto Union with the engine in the front, but the body was equally sleek with the front suspension enclosed. The engine was a 3.3-litre, supercharged straight eight which developed a massive 314 bhp.

The Type A and the W25 both used light alloys for the engine castings wherever possible, and lightweight tubes to make the chassis. They met the requirements of the new formula but, whatever the intention of the AIACR, were clearly much faster and more powerful than any of their rivals.

Both cars were scheduled to make their debuts at the Avus track near Berlin on 27 May 1934, but Mercedes pulled out after carburettor problems during practice and it was three Auto Unions, driven by Hans Stuck, August Momberger and Prince Hermann zu Leiningen, which were paraded before the Führer and 200,000 German spectators. The opposition came from Scuderia Ferrari Alfas driven by Guy Moll and Chiron. Stuck and Leiningen retired with mechanical problems and Momberger was third behind the two Alfas.

ABOVE Rudolf Caracciola more than any other driver fulfilled the Führer's mission for German racing drivers: he won 26 major Grands Prix and was European Champion in 1935, 1937 and 1938.

BELOW Line-up at the Nürburgring for the Eifel Grand Prix in 1937: Bernd Rosemeyer, No. 1, Auto Union (winner); Manfred von Brauchitsch No. 8, Mercedes (third); Caracciola, No. 6 Mercedes (second). Nuvolari, No. 11 on the third row of the grid, is driving the unsuccessful Alfa Romeo 12C-37.

RIGHT The cockpit of the Mercedes W154/163: the steering wheel was removable to allow access and egress for the drivers. In 1939, that feature contributed to the death of Richard Seaman. He crashed into a tree and was knocked unconscious; a fuel pipe was broken and the car caught fire. The marshals were unable to release the steering wheel before he had been very severely burnt, and he died later in hospital.

BELOW The man behind the cars: Rudolf Uhlenhaut was Technical Director at Mercedes during their years at the top from 1936 to 1939. He joined the company as an engineer to work on passenger cars, but once he became involved in the racing department, he learnt high speed driving so that he could test the cars himself.

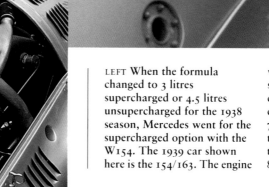

LEFT When the formula changed to 3 litres supercharged or 4.5 litres unsupercharged for the 1938 season, Mercedes went for the supercharged option with the W154. The 1939 car shown here is the 154/163. The engine was a 2962 cc, V-12 with twin superchargers, twin overhead camshafts and four valves per cylinder. It gave 484 bhp at 7500 rpm, but it was very thirsty – a gallon of fuel every two miles; the fuel tank held 88 gallons.

MERCEDES: THE SILVER ARROWS

ver since the days of the Gordon Bennett races, Germany's racing colour had been white, but at the first outing of the Mercedes W25 in 1934, Alfred Neubauer ordered all the paint to be stripped off to comply with the weight limit. The highly polished aluminium looked like silver and subsequently the colour was adopted officially and gave the team its unofficial name. The Mercedes team of drivers in the late 1930s – Rudolf Caracciola, Hermann Lang, Richard Seaman and Manfred von Brauchitsch – were among the best that could be found, but their success was built on a formidable team structure which included the manager Alfred Neubauer who enforced strict rules on the drivers on the tactics to be used in the race. If one of the team was leading well, the other drivers were under orders not to put pressure on him by driving too close and put at risk a Mercedes victory for the sake of a personal triumph.

BELOW French Grand Prix 1938: von Brauchitsch, the eventual winner, among the cornfields of the Reims circuit. Mercedes filled the first three places.

Two weeks later both German teams were at the Nürburgring for the Eifel Grand Prix. The Mercedes cars were 1 kg over the weight limit, so the team manager, Alfred Neubauer, had all the paint stripped off to bring them within it. Mercedes' drivers were Manfred von Brauchitsch and Fagioli. The latter went into the lead followed by von Brauchitsch, and so it stayed for the early part of the race. With victory seemingly assured, Neubauer decided that it should be a German driver who won, and signalled Fagioli to let his team-mate pass. Fagioli complied but was furious. A fierce row ensued in the pits and Fagioli stormed off, leaving von Brauchitsch to win from Stuck in the Auto Union.

The French Grand Prix had in the past seen France humiliated by Germany and on 1 July the grandstands at Montlhéry were 'seething with excitement' (according to _The Autocar_) as the start approached. There were five teams: Mercedes with von Brauchitsch, Fagioli and Caracciola, who was still only barely fit after his accident in the 1933 Monaco Grand Prix; Auto Union had Stuck and Momberger; Scuderia Ferrari had three P.3s driven by Chiron, Varzi and Count Felice Trossi; Nuvolari and Robert Benoist were driving Bugattis and Maserati had Zehender and Etancelin.

The Mercedes were fastest in practice, but at the start Chiron shot forward from the second row of the grid to take the lead on the first lap from Caracciola and Fagioli followed by Stuck. On the second lap, Stuck got past the two Mercedes to challenge Chiron who, although driving an Italian car, was the favourite with the French crowd. On the third lap, Stuck took the lead leaving Chiron to battle with the two Mercedes. So it went on for nine laps until Stuck's car gave him trouble and Chiron took the lead again with Caracciola and Fagioli still just behind. Lap records fell as the battle went on, but gradually all the German cars retired with mechanical problems leaving the race to the three Alfas. The P.3s were the only cars to finish the race: Chiron ahead of Varzi and Moll, who had taken over from Trossi. A Frenchman had won. The defeat of 1914 had been avenged. The crowd was ecstatic.

It was a famous victory for the P.3s, but they were not really up to the German cars. A new era was at hand: Mercedes and Auto Union shared most of the honours for the rest of 1934. Stuck won the German, Swiss and Czech Grands Prix for Auto Union. Fagioli won the Spanish for Mercedes, and Caracciola upset the Italians by winning their Grand Prix for Mercedes.

The German cars had breathed new life into Grand Prix racing, and in 1935 a European Championship for drivers was introduced. Mercedes and Auto Union had ironed out most of their mechanical problems and made their engines even bigger: Auto Union increased its size to nearly 5 litres (4950 cc) at which it developed 375 bhp. Mercedes increased theirs to just under 4 litres to produce 435 bhp. Against this, the ageing P.3 Alfas were bored out to 3165 cc giving them 265 bhp. For Mercedes, Caracciola won the French, Swiss, Belgian and Spanish Grands Prix and Fagioli won the Italian at Monza; Stuck won the Monaco for Auto Union.

With such dominance, German racing fans (and Hitler) confidently expected that one of the two German cars would win the German Grand Prix at the Nürburgring in 1935. Mercedes still had its winning team of Caracciola, von Brauchitsch and Fagioli. Auto Union still had its star, Stuck, supported by Bernd Rosemeyer, who had previously raced motor cycles. Nuvolari had wanted a place on the Auto Union team, but it had gone to Varzi, his arch rival. Nuvolari was driving a specially prepared Scuderia Alfa P.3 which had been bored out to 3.8 litres giving about 330 bhp.

Caracciola went into the lead but, astonishingly, Nuvolari was only 12 seconds behind him at the end of the first lap. He was quickly overtaken by Rosemeyer and Fagioli, and Chiron in another

RIGHT Survivor from 1939: the Mercedes W154 driven by Neil Corner at Silverstone in 1990. The 3-litre engine used a methanol fuel mixture including nitro-benzene, and developed 497 bhp. This car, driven by Hermann Lang, was timed at 197 mph at Spa in Belgium in 1939. It was hidden in Czechoslovakia during the war and raced at Indianapolis in 1948/1949 by Tommy Lee. It took 10 years to restore the car to its present condition. W154s driven by Hermann Lang, Manfred von Brauchitsch and Rudolf Caracciola won 12 of the 18 major Grands Prix in 1938/1939.

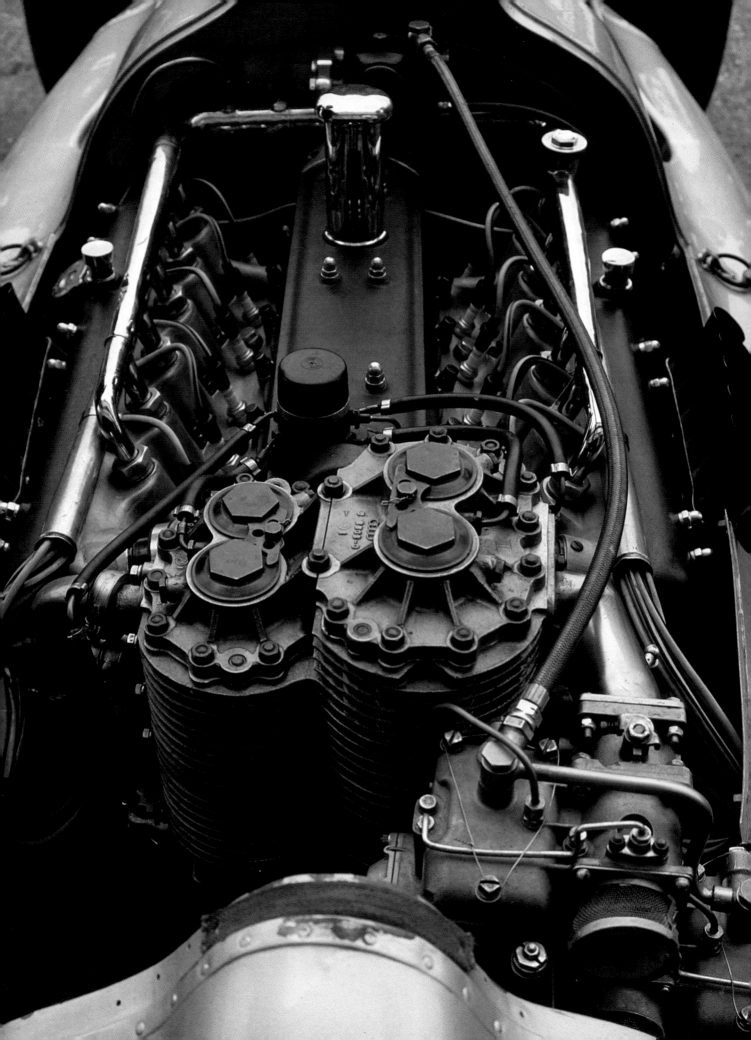

Alfa. The predicted battle – between Mercedes, represented by Caracciola, and Auto Union, represented by Rosemeyer – looked to be the pattern for the race, but by lap 10 Nuvolari had worked his way through the field again and passed Caracciola into the lead. A bad pit stop cost him six places but he set out again, as grimly determined as ever. Von Brauchitsch was now leading followed by Stuck, Caracciola, Rosemeyer and Fagioli. Nuvolari, driving like a man possessed in the obsolete P.3, worked his way through to second place. As they went into the final lap, he was just 30 seconds behind von Brauchitsch. The German driver's lead should have been enough, but to stay ahead he had been giving his tyres a battering; with less than half a lap to go, one burst. Nuvolari crossed the line to win before a sullen German crowd. He was followed by Stuck, Caracciola, Rosemeyer and then von Brauchitsch driving on three tyres and one wheel rim.

Nuvolari's win remains one of the greatest victories of all time, but it was the P.3's swansong. The German cars were clearly dominant and Caracciola had won enough points to become European Champion.

Between them Mercedes and Auto Union remained unbeatable. In 1936, Auto Union swept the board with Rosemeyer, in only his second season, becoming European Champion. The 750-kg formula was extended for the 1937 season and the German cars swept the board again, Caracciola becoming World Champion for a second time. Not only did Mercedes and Auto Union win, the record shows hardly any other cars in the first three places of any major race. In 1937, Mercedes brought out the W125 with a massive 5.6-litre engine which produced 570 bhp, and a version of the W25 which gave nearly 600 bhp. Speeds began to reach 200 mph.

The AIACR acted. For 1938, after a decade of formulae based on anything but engine size, they limited supercharged cars to 3 litres and unsupercharged ones to 4.5 litres. Mercedes brought out the 3-litre W154 which, by 1939, was producing 485 bhp. Auto Union reached a similar output.

The French Grand Prix was the traditional battleground between France and Germany. In the

Last of the line: the Auto Union Type D (ABOVE) is driven by World Champion John Surtees at Silverstone in 1990. Only five were built and this is the last running example. The 3-litre Type D V-12 engine (OPPOSITE) developed 385 bhp at 4500 rpm. Tazio Nuvolari drove a Type D to victory in the Yugoslavian Grand Prix on 3 September 1939 – the day war broke out.

BELOW Bernd Rosemeyer in an Auto Union Type C in practice for the 1937 British Grand Prix at Donington, which he won. He was killed on 26 January 1938 on the Darmstadt/Frankfurt autobahn driving an Auto Union in a speed-record attempt.

ABOVE The Mercedes team at the Swiss Grand Prix 1938. From left to right: Rudolf Uhlenhaut (technical director), Manfred von Brauchitsch (third), Rudolf Caracciola (winner), Richard Seaman (second), Max Sailer (veteran driver and director of Daimler-Benz) and Alfred Neubauer (team manager).

RIGHT *Deutschland über alles*: streamlined cars at the Avus track in 1937.

OPPOSITE Germany's triumph in motor racing is celebrated at the Berlin Motor Show in 1939. The propaganda value of the German government's involvement in motor racing was the subject of a British Secret Service report after the war.

years up to the outbreak of the Second World War, von Brauchitsch won in 1937 and 1938, Mercedes taking the first three places in both races, and Otto Müller won in 1939 in an Auto Union with Georg Meier in second place in another. History had more than repeated itself.

Alfa Romeo licked its wounds. Jano had been given the task of building a Grand-Prix car to challenge the might of Germany, but his 12C-37 was a failure and he was sacked after 15 years service. Alfa Romeo brought racing back under its own roof with Ferrari now managing Alfa Corse (Alfa Racing) rather than his own team. With Ferrari's encouragement, Gioachino Colombo, the new designer, concentrated on the 1.5-litre voiturette class, building the Alfa 158, a super-charged, 8-cylinder, 195-bhp single-seater. The 1939 Tripoli Grand Prix was run under the voiturette formula and it looked as if the Alfa star

might rise again. But Mercedes sent over two V-8 1.5-litre W165 cars. Driven by Hermann Lang and Caracciola, they came first and second; Emilio Villoresi was third in the 158.

In September 1939 Europe was at war again. There was no racing except in Italy which stayed out of the conflict until 1940. Tripoli was an Italian colony and the Grand Prix was run there in 1940 under the 1.5-litre formula. Alfa 158s came first, second and third. Racing stopped completely once Italy was in the war and the 158s were put into storage. When the Germans took over the country in 1943, Alfa Romeo, fearful that they might be requisitioned or used as scrap, walled them up inside a cheese factory to wait for the peace.

—CHAPTER FIVE—
WORLD CHAMPIONS

Six years of war reduced the automobile industries of the combatant nations of Europe to a parlous state. Factories had again been harnessed for munitions or military-vehicle production and many had been flattened by bombs. But some racing cars had survived and drivers and spectators were eager for races to be held. The war ended on 8 May 1945. On 9 September Paris reasserted its position as the centre of the sport by holding the first post-war race meeting in the Bois de Boulogne. There was a poignant echo of the conflict in the names chosen for the three races: the Robert Benoist Trophy in memory of the pre-war driver who had served in the Resistance and was hanged by the Gestapo; the Liberation Trophy; and the Coupe des Prisonniers. The winners were Amedée Gordini in a car made from Simca and Fiat parts, Henry Louveau in a Maserati and Jean-Pierre Wimille in a Type 59 Bugatti. It was a moment of colour in an otherwise drab post-war landscape.

Competitive cars were in short supply and it was going to take some time to re-establish racing at Grand Prix level. Germany was banned and in any case few of their pre-war titans had survived. Britain's ERAs had survived, but were long in the tooth and underpowered for Grand Prix racing. The French company Talbot-Lago, which had produced sports cars and single-seaters before the war, started working on a 4.5-litre single-seater.

The Italians were in a much better position. Maserati had several examples of their pre-war

LEFT **Post-war supremo: the Alfa 158. Built as a voiturette before the Second World War, it was the backbone of Grand Prix racing between 1946 and 1951.**

1.5-litre, supercharged voiturette, the 4CLT, and Alfa Romeo took the 158s from their hide-out in the cheese factory and dusted them off for a new lease of life. Alfa secured a team of five drivers: Dr (of law) Giuseppe 'Nino' Farina, Count Felice Trossi, Jean-Pierre Wimille, Consalvo Sanesi and the venerable Achille Varzi, who had managed to kick a morphine addiction to return to racing.

There were only four Grands Prix in 1946. The first one was on the outskirts of Paris at St Cloud

ABOVE Alfa 158: the name '158' derived from the 1.5-litre engine which had eight cylinders; they were affectionately known as 'Alfettas', 'little Alfas', from their pre-war status as voiturettes.

LEFT Post-war poster: motor racing looks to the future at the Grand Prix des Nations in Switzerland in 1946.

BELOW Jean-Pierre Wimille ahead of Achille Varzi at Geneva in 1946; both are driving Alfa Romeo 158s.

where the Alfas had to retire, leaving the race to Raymond Sommer in a Maserati. Then came the second Grand Prix des Nations in Switzerland which Farina won with Trossi second and Wimille third. Alfa then won the other two, minor, Italian events and it was clear that it would be the car to beat in 1947 when Grand Prix racing would return in full. The Fédération Internationale d'Automobiles (FIA), formed in 1946 to organize the sport at an international level, set a formula for 1947 which could encompass what cars were available: either 1.5-litre supercharged or 4.5-litre unsupercharged.

Alfa won every race it entered that year, filling the first three places in the Swiss, Belgian and Italian Grands Prix: Wimille won the first two and Trossi the Italian event. Alfa did not contest the

French race, which was won by Louis Chiron in a Talbot, but any respite for French fans was temporary. The Alfa team came to Reims in 1948 putting the Talbots back to fourth place behind Wimille, Trossi and a new driver, Alberto Ascari, son of the famous Antonio Ascari, who came third in his only drive for his father's old firm. It was a triumphal year for Alfa: it won every race it entered. But it was also a sad time: Varzi was killed in practice for the Swiss Grand Prix and Wimille died tragically during a minor race in Argentina in January 1949 when trying to avoid spectators who had strayed on to the track.

Other cars got a look in only when Alfa were not there. The first post-war British Grand Prix was held in 1948 on the disused wartime airfield at Silverstone. Ten out of the 18 entries were pre-war ERAs and Chiron was there in a Talbot, but Italy triumphed nevertheless: Luigi Villoresi and Ascari came first and second in their Maseratis ahead of an ERA driven by Bob Gerard.

At the Italian Grand Prix that year, there was a new Italian name on the starting-grid alongside Alfa and Maserati – Ferrari. On parting with Alfa before the war, Enzo Ferrari had agreed not to race as Scuderia Ferrari for four years. He turned to general automobile engineering and during the war secured some lucrative government contracts. After 1945 he returned to racing and decided to do so on his own. He approached Gioachino Colombo, his ex-Alfa colleague and designer of the 158. Colombo wanted to build a mid-engined car on the lines of a prewar prototype Alfa Romeo, the 152, but Ferrari vetoed the idea, remarking that the horse goes in front of the cart. The Ferrari 125 reflected his conservatism in matters of design: the 225-bhp, 1.5-litre supercharged V-12 engine was in the front.

With two of their drivers dead and the company in financial trouble again, Alfa withdrew from the Grand Prix circuit for 1949. In Alfa's absence Maserati, Ferrari and Talbot had some success: Louis Rosier won the Belgian Grand Prix in a Talbot, from Villoresi in the new Ferrari. Chiron won the French Grand Prix for Talbot with Maserati second and Ferrari third. Ascari gave Ferrari victory in the Italian Grand Prix.

ABOVE **Juan Manuel Fangio** was born in 1911 in Argentina where he started racing as a riding mechanic.

ABOVE RIGHT **Italian Grand Prix, Monza 1957**: on this occasion Fangio came second to Stirling Moss in a Vanwall. Fangio raced in 51 World Championship events, of which he won 24.

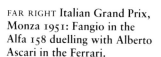

FAR RIGHT **Italian Grand Prix, Monza 1951**: Fangio in the Alfa 158 duelling with Alberto Ascari in the Ferrari.

RIGHT **German Grand Prix, Nürburgring 1957**: Fangio at the wheel of his Maserati 250F during the drive of his life.

THE MAESTRO

Juan Manuel Fangio is the only driver to have won the World Drivers' Championship five times: 1951, 1954, 1955, 1956, 1957. He clinched his final title with one of the legendary drives in motor-racing history at the Nürburgring. It was a victory of sublime skill triumphing over a plan which went wrong. He was driving a Maserati 250F and his main opponents were Peter Collins and Mike Hawthorn, both in Ferraris.

He knew that he would have to stop for tyres during the race, which the Ferraris should be able to complete without stopping, so took on just enough fuel to make it to the pit stop. This meant his car was lighter at the start and he intended to build up a good lead. He was 30 seconds ahead when he made his stop on lap 12, but the pits took 52 seconds during which Collins and Hawthorn went into first and second positions. Back on the track, Fangio was 45 seconds behind. By lap 20 he had narrowed the gap to 2 seconds, having broken the lap record several times in the process. He passed Collins and then Hawthorn. Fangio won by 3.6 seconds. After the race, he said that he never wanted to do what he had done to win the event again.

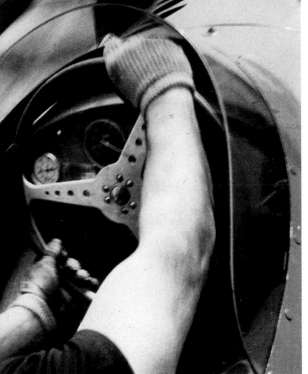

ABOVE AND RIGHT **Alberto Ascari's Ferrari 500 in which he won six World Championship Grands Prix in 1952 and five in 1953. He was World Champion in both years that the Championship was run under Formula Two. The car is preserved at the Donington Museum in Derbyshire. The 190-bhp 2-litre engine was designed by Aurelio Lampredi.**

In 1950, motor racing started the new decade in an expansionist mood. A third formula was introduced for 500-cc cars bringing the sport within the range of more people. Germany came back into the fold of racing nations with its own Grand Prix which Ascari won for Ferrari. In Britain, the first post-war Tourist Trophy race was held; it was won by a new British driver, Stirling Moss, in a Jaguar. ERA was reincarnated as British Racing Motors (BRM), a patriotic consortium of industrialists headed by Raymond Mays. It produced a V-16, supercharged, 1.5-litre single-seater which was immensely powerful. There were great expectations for the car, but when it appeared at Silverstone later that year it broke down on the starting line.

The most exciting development was the introduction of a World Championship for drivers. Points were awarded for performance in seven races: the British, Swiss, Monaco, Belgian, ACF and Italian Grands Prix and the Indianapolis 500.

The inclusion of the American classic was an attempt to forge transatlantic links in motor racing and bring together the worlds of oval-track and

road racing. Both had long and very different traditions and they produced very different types of cars. During the 1930s, the 'Junk Formula', based on 'stock' engine blocks, had been introduced at Indianapolis to encourage the American automobile industry back into racing. But Harry Miller's legacy of superbly designed racing engines had not died with his bankruptcy in 1933. His two lieutenants, Fred Offenhauser and Leo Goosen, continued to produce Miller engines. These Offenhauser Millers had their first victory at Indianapolis in 1935 and continued to win until 1938. For use in midget racing cars, Offenhauser built a smaller 4-cylinder engine which became known as the Offenhauser, or 'Offy'. After the war, Offenhauser sold the business, but the new owners continued to produce the engines. Cars at Indianapolis were usually known by the name of their sponsors, but well into the 1960s these 'roadsters' were invariably powered by an 'Offy' engine in a chassis built by a

specialist designer. Two designers, Frank Kurtis and A. J. Watson, built most of the winning cars, and built them specifically to win at Indianapolis – even offsetting the engines to one side to help them in the corners, which were all in the same direction.

During the Depression and through the war, the fabric of the Indianapolis Speedway had suffered from neglect, but in 1945 it was extensively renovated by a new owner, Tony Hulman, a businessman with a vision of what it should be and the money to back his vision. However, the speedway remained isolated from developments elsewhere in the world and very few drivers from Europe raced there, even after the Indianapolis 500 was included in the World Drivers' Championship.

The first race to count for that Championship was the 1950 British Grand Prix at Silverstone. It was a grand affair: the FIA awarded it the honorary title of Grand Prix d'Europe and George VI and Queen Elizabeth, attended by the band of the

Grenadier Guards, were present. Motor racing took on the status of a cup final or a test match.

Alfa Romeo was there: once the World Championship was at stake, the company could not pick and choose which races to attend. The 158 had been boosted to 350 bhp and Alfa had a strong team: Farina, Luigi Fagioli and Juan Manuel Fangio, an Argentinian driver who had been racing in Europe backed by money from his government and by Argentinian motor clubs. Alfa thoughtfully

BELOW LEFT Italian dominance: Alberto Ascari and Piero Taruffi at Silverstone in July 1952. Ascari had just won the British Grand Prix for Ferrari, and Taruffi the *Daily Express* Formula Libre Trophy. Taruffi's car was a 'Thin Wall Special', a 4.5-litre Ferrari entered by the industrialist Tony Vandervell who manufactured Thin Wall bearings and later went on to build the successful Vanwall racing cars of the late 1950s.

RIGHT Taruffi in the rain at the 1951 Swiss Grand Prix, where he was second to Fangio in an Alfa 158.

BELOW Ascari on his way to victory in the Ferrari 500 in the Belgian Grand Prix of 1952.

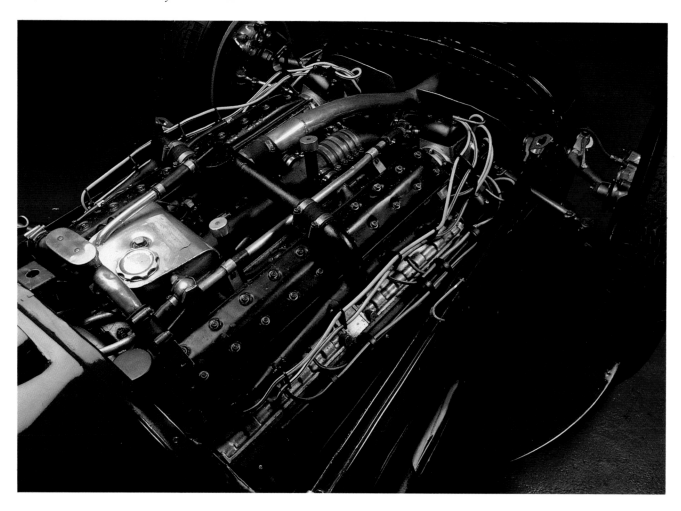

provided a car for a British driver, Reg Parnell, giving the host country a chance to win. Fangio had to retire, but it was still an Alfa procession: Farina won with Fagioli second and Parnell third.

For the Italian Grand Prix, Alfa boosted the power of the 158 to 370 bhp. Ferrari had given up the 1.5-litre supercharged engine in favour of a 4.5-litre unsupercharged one. He had parted company with Colombo and taken on another designer, Aurelio Lampredi, who had designed a new V-12 engine for the new car. At 340 bhp, the 375 was less powerful than the Alfa, but it was also less complex and had one crucial advantage: it had to make only one fuel stop for every two required by the 158 – as a result of raising the power of the 158's engine, fuel consumption had increased to the point where it was only giving around 2 miles to the gallon. Farina won the Italian event for Alfa, but Ascari gave him a hard time in the Ferrari and

ABOVE **False start: the V-16 engine. It was immensely powerful, but over-complicated, and the BRM never won any of the Grands Prix it was designed for. The supercharger used a centrifugal compressor designed by Rolls-Royce.**

ABOVE RIGHT **Raymond Mays (1899–1980) at the wheel of the first BRM in 1950. The car was a failure, but the idea he sowed – that Britain should be among the leaders in Grand Prix racing – caught on and British designers and builders of racing cars were in the forefront of the business.**

came second. Alfas won all six World Championship events that year and Farina became World Champion. The 158s were nevertheless entering the autumn of their years.

The opening race of the 1951 season was once again the British Grand Prix. The line-up was formidable: Alfa had boosted the 158 still further, to 420 bhp, and laced the fuel with alcohol. Alfa had four drivers: Fangio, Farina, Sanesi and a new man, Felice Bonetto. The Ferrari 375s were driven by Ascari, Villoresi and another Argentinian, Froilan

Gonzalez. There were two BRMs driven by Parnell and Peter Walker. The race was a titanic struggle between the two Argentinians, Fangio and Gonzalez, driving two Italian cars, the pre-war 1.5-litre Alfa and the new 4.5-litre Ferrari. Gonzalez went into an early lead, but by lap 10 Fangio had used up some of the heavy fuel load and overtook him. By lap 25, Fangio was 6 seconds ahead, but Gonzalez managed to haul it back to 2 seconds. Then Ascari had to retire. As senior Ferrari driver he could have taken Gonzalez' car, but he sportingly waived this right. Gonzalez went on to drive the race of his life and beat Fangio by 51 seconds.

Alfa had been beaten; it was the beginning of the end for the 1.5-litre supercharged car. The event was a triumph for Ferrari, who was now on the map as a producer of Formula One cars. But the Alfas went out fighting: they and Ferrari both won three World Championship events, but Fangio fin-ished ahead on points to become the second World Champion. Nothing more could be squeezed out of the venerable 158 and Alfa pulled out of racing after 30 years and three memorable cars: the P.2 and the P.3 before the war and the 158.

The race also saw the end of the much-vaunted V-16 BRM. Parnell and Walker finished fifth and seventh, placings that were highly creditable: the drivers were burnt by the heat of the exhaust pipes and stifled by fuel vapour. The BRM was unreliable and very tricky to handle. The engine ultimately produced 440 bhp – 293 bhp/litre; the problem was putting that power to effective use. The car was prone to wheel spin when the full power was used through the narrow tyres.

With Alfa out of racing and BRM not meeting expectations, Ferrari was the only team with a competitive car for the 1952 season. The World Championship was run using Formula Two cars: 2

litres unsupercharged or 500 cc supercharged. This did not hinder Ferrari, who had a Formula Two car ready. In 1952 and 1953, Ferrari won 30 out of 33 races entered; Ascari won 19 and was World Champion in both years.

The new formula in 1954 – 2.5 litres unsupercharged or 750 cc supercharged – produced a crop of new cars although hardly anybody went for the unsupercharged option. Ferrari brought out the 625 with a straight 4-cylinder engine which gave 210 bhp at 7000 rpm. Maserati was back with the 250F. Colombo had a hand in the original design of this beautiful car, which had a straight 6-cylinder engine giving 240 bhp at 7200 rpm. There was a Maserati team, but cars were also sold to private entrants, one of whom was Stirling Moss.

Lancia returned to racing with a new car designed by Vittorio Jano. The D50's V-8 engine was slightly offset, allowing the drive shaft to pass down the left of the cockpit. It was also a structural member of the chassis – rather than sitting in the chassis, it was part of the chassis. Externally, its most distinctive feature was the fuel tanks, thin panniers slung outside the body between the wheels. Most cars of the period had a large fuel tank in the rear and as a race progressed the weight distribution changed and with it the handling; the D50's layout avoided this.

The sensation of the year was Mercedes' return to Grand Prix racing after 15 years. Its W196 looked more like a sports car with its wheels enclosed in a streamlined body. Typically, Mercedes had been thorough in the preparation of its cars. It had also been innovative: the engine was a straight eight, but it was inclined at 20 degrees to the horizontal, so that the general layout of the car could be kept as low as possible; it had fuel injection and desmodromic valve operation. (Instead of a cam to open the valve and a spring to return it, the valve was opened and closed by the positive action of the cam.) This enabled Mercedes eventually to go to 8000 rpm giving 260 bhp.

RIGHT **End of an era: one of the last of the front-engined racing cars, the beautiful Maserati 250F, originally conceived by Gioachino Colombo. From the 1960s on, racing-car designers looked to function rather than form.**

VANWALL

Guy Anthony Vandervell (1896–1967) was one of the architects of the development of a British racing car industry in the 1950s. He came from a wealthy family and, as a young man, raced motorcycles and cars in the 1920s. In 1930 he saw the potential in an American method of making bearings for car engines. They were 'shells' on to which a thin coating of bearing metal had been deposited, making them removable and much cheaper to change when they wore out. He bought a licence to produce them in Britain and before long he was supplying most of the British motor industry. After the war, he was drawn into the BRM project. He bought a Type 125 Ferrari which he called the Thin Wall Special which gave BRM a car in which to gain experience. Then he went out on his own to achieve his real objective which was to build a car to beat the Italians. In this he succeeded, providing a springboard for the nascent British racing car industry.

ABOVE **British dominance: Tony Brooks in a Vanwall leading Fangio in a Maserati, hotly pursued by Moss and Stuart Lewis-Evans in two more Vanwalls at the Italian Grand Prix at Monza in 1957.**

RIGHT **Survivors of the 1950s: a Vanwall, driven by Alain de Cadenet, holding off a Maserati 250F, driven by Neil Corner, in an historic Grand Prix car race at Silverstone in 1990.**

LEFT **A great British moment: Stirling Moss in a Vanwall, winning the British Grand Prix at Aintree in 1957.**

The time and place of the unveiling of the W196 was chosen with care. It was the French Grand Prix at Reims on 4 July 1954 – 40 years and one day after Mercedes had humiliated Peugeot in 1914. The team consisted of Fangio, Karl Kling and Hans Hermann. Fangio and Kling were on the front row of the grid next to Ascari in a Maserati 250F. Ascari had been contracted to drive the Lancia D50 but it was not yet ready, so he had been lent to Maserati. Gonzalez was driving for Ferrari. Mercedes, Maserati and Ferrari filled the first 14 places on the starting grid.

Fangio and Kling shot away from the grid with only Gonzalez managing to stay in touch with the two Mercedes. By lap five his tenacity was slipping and he had dropped 7 seconds behind and was being challenged by Hermann in the third Mercedes. With Fangio and Kling out in front a fierce battle for third place developed between Gonzalez and Herrmann. Herrmann managed to get past and Gonzalez, trying hard to repass him, spun dangerously at the Thillois hairpin, his engine already smoking; he retired shortly afterwards. But the strain had shown on Hermann's car too; by lap 17 smoke was pouring from it and he retired. The two remaining Mercedes stage-managed their finish with Fangio winning from Kling by a 10th of a second. Fangio stormed through the rest of the season and earned his second World Championship.

The following year, 1955, was a sad one. A Mercedes sports car crashed at Le Mans killing over 80 spectators and casting a shadow of gloom over motor racing. The French Grand Prix, among other races, was cancelled. Ascari had been killed testing a car at Monza. Lancia found the financial strain of maintaining a top team too much and pulled out, handing over the D50s to Ferrari. Mercedes had a successful year and Fangio took his third World Champion title, but the company pulled out of racing, giving as their reason the sport's drain on research and development skills and resources which were needed for their passenger cars. Moss went to Maserati; Fangio went to Ferrari where, in 1956, he won his fourth World title driving the D50.

Except for the brief surge by Mercedes, Formula One racing had been dominated by Italian cars since the war, but in the same period, Britain had been stirring. BRM had been a failure, but it provided a boost to the idea that British cars could compete at the top level. Tony Vandervell had been part of the BRM project, but had become disenchanted with the committee approach of the BRM management. He decided to build his own all-British racing car, the Vanwall.

Unlike the huge, integrated German firms like Daimler-Benz, Britain's industry was based on a great many small engineering businesses, many of them specialists, and it was to them that Vandervell turned. He was a director of Norton Motor Cycles and looked to them to design a 4-cylinder engine based on their motor cycles. For the 1956 season Vandervell asked Colin Chapman to design a new chassis and Charles and John Cooper, a father and son in the garage business in Surrey, who had been building Formula Three cars since just after the war, built the prototype. Stirling Moss drove the new car at the International Trophy meeting at

LEFT Stirling Moss driving his T51 Cooper-Climax at Monaco in 1959. He started in pole position and led for most of the race until his transmission broke. Jack Brabham won in another Cooper and went on to win the World Championship that year.

BELOW Formula Three, V-2, 500-cc Cooper at the Prescott Hill Climb in 1954: the original Coopers were built from parts scrounged from war-surplus dumps and scrapyards.

Silverstone and won, and at the 1956 French Grand Prix, Harry Schell in a Vanwall gave the Lancia-Ferraris of Fangio and Peter Collins a real fight.

For the 1957 season, Chapman had a new, more aerodynamically efficient body designed by Frank Costin and the engine was boosted to 275 bhp making the Vanwall the most powerful Grand Prix car. At the British Grand Prix at Aintree, there were three Vanwalls driven by Moss, Brooks and Stuart Lewis-Evans; four Maseratis driven by Fangio, Schell, Carlos Menditeguy and Jean Behra; and four Lancia-Ferraris driven by Mike Hawthorn and Peter Collins, with Luigi Musso and the French driver Maurice Trintignant. BRM, now under the direction of Sir Alfred Owen of the Owen Organization, had produced a new car, the P25; two were on the grid driven by Les Leston and Jack Fairman. There were also three mid-engined Coopers with 1.96-litre Coventry Climax engines, driven by the Australian driver Jack Brabham, and by Roy Salvadori and Bob Gerard.

Moss and Brooks were in the front row of the grid with Behra, in front of Fangio and Hawthorn. Moss went into the lead and began to draw steadily away from Hawthorn and Behra. Brooks was fourth in the other Vanwall. An all-British victory looked possible, then Moss's engine started misfiring. He called into the pits and the mechanics tried to fix it but to no avail; he came in again on lap 26. The team manager then signalled Brooks,

who was lying ninth, to come in and hand over to Moss. Behra was leading followed by Hawthorn with Lewis-Evans third. Fangio retired with engine failure; Behra's clutch failed and Hawthorn had a puncture, leaving the two Vanwalls lying first and second until Lewis-Evans' throttle linkage broke putting Moss back in the lead. The crowd erupted in ecstasy when he crossed the line to win after 90 laps – a British driver, driving a British car, had won a Grand Prix, the first time since Henry Seagrave won at Tours in the Sunbeam in 1923.

Vandervell had set out to beat the Italians, and he had done it. Over the next two years, Vanwalls put Britain on the motor racing map; they became the cars to beat. In 1958, Vanwall, with Moss, Brooks and Lewis-Evans in the team, won six of the 10 World Championship races to take the newly formed World Constructors' Championship. Moss won four Grands Prix that year, the last one in Morocco, but the World Champion title went to Hawthorn driving for Ferrari. He had won only one Grand Prix but had accumulated more points than Moss with second and third places.

ABOVE **Formula Three Coopers at Aintree in 1955: at their peak, Cooper was producing these cars at the rate of more than one a week.**

RIGHT **Cockpit of the Cooper T43. Roy Salvadori came fifth in this car in the British Grand Prix in 1957, giving Cooper its first World Championship points in the 2.5-litre Formula.**

PAGES 150–1 **Classic Coopers: No. 10 (foreground) is Salvadori's 1957 T43; No. 1 (rear) is one of two works T53s made for the 1960 season. It was Bruce McLaren's car; Jack Brabham became World Champion, for the second time, in the other T53.**

A new British star seemed to be rising; Vanwall had won nine of the 14 Grands Prix it had entered. But it was not to be: at the end of 1958, Vandervell pulled the team out of Grand Prix racing after Lewis-Evans' death following a crash in Morocco.

While Vanwall had been storming to victory Charles Cooper and his son John, the men who had built the first model, had been making progress. They had prospered through the 1950s, building Formula Two and Formula Three cars in which many British drivers such as Hawthorn learnt their trade.

Their first foray into Formula One came in 1955 at the British Grand Prix with Jack Brabham but

he was unplaced. In the 1957 Monaco Grand Prix, Brabham was lying third in a T41 Formula Two Cooper with a 2-litre engine when a fuel pump mounting broke and he had to push his car over the line for a sixth place. That same year, Salvadori gained fifth place in the famous British Grand Prix in a T43 Cooper.

In 1958, special fuel mixtures were outlawed and ordinary fuel made mandatory. Maserati pulled out of the Argentinian Grand Prix in Buenos Aires, although a car was sent for Fangio and there were plenty of private Maserati entrants. Ferrari was there with a new car, the 246 'Dino', named after Enzo's son Alfredino who had a hand in its design before dying of muscular dystrophy in 1956. Its V-6 engine which gave 280 bhp at 8300 rpm had been designed by Jano. The drivers were Musso and Hawthorn.

Vanwall was not there because the race, the first of the season, had been included too late for it to be ready, so there was only a single British entry: Stirling Moss in a Cooper T43, painted blue for Scotland since it was entered by the private Rob Walker team. Its 1.96-litre engine gave 175 bhp. This was 100 bhp less than the Ferraris, but the Italian cars were much heavier so the power-to-weight ratio was roughly equal. However, the Cooper had better acceleration and better braking, it was lower and, because it was smaller, it had less wind resistance.

The Maseratis did not do well on the lower-grade fuel and the race quickly resolved into a battle between Moss in the Cooper and the Ferraris of Musso and Hawthorn. Moss took the lead, but the two Ferrari drivers did not press too hard: they believed he would have to go into the pits for a tyre change, and they had already done so. But Moss had other ideas; his pits prepared for a change but he drove on, conserving his tyres as much as possible by careful driving. Too late, it dawned on Musso, who was lying second, that Moss was not going in for tyres. Moss won with the canvas showing through.

It was a famous drive for Moss and a triumph for Rob Walker – the first time a privately entered car had won a World Championship event. It was

AMERICA'S FIRST WORLD CHAMPION

Phil Hill started his racing career in sports cars in America, a type of racing much closer to the European road-racing tradition. In 1958, he drove in a Grand Prix for the first time, for Maserati, and was later signed by Ferrari as a works driver. In 1961, Ferrari's top drivers were Hill and Wolfgang von Trips who was poised to become World Champion; Hill was behind him on points. Both were driving the Dino 246. The penultimate race of the season was the Italian Grand Prix at Monza. Winning it would clinch the title for von Trips, but he collided with Jim Clark's Lotus, crashed and was killed. Hill went on to win the race and with it the Championship. He continued to drive until 1967.

RIGHT **Phil Hill in 1961: he was born in 1927.**

LEFT Monaco 1959: Phil Hill in a Ferrari 246.

BELOW Monaco 1961: Hill passing the Hôtel de Paris.

ABOVE Ferrari 1961: Hill's victory in the Italian Grand Prix that year gave him the World Championship; it was the last Grand Prix victory in a rear-engined car.

also the first time for a mid-engined car. The Coopers were ideal for the twisting Monaco circuit and Trintignant won that event soon afterwards.

Britain was on top in 1958. It had been Vanwall's year but as Vandervell withdrew, Cooper picked up the torch. The 1959 season was between the Cooper, which now had a 2.5-litre engine, and the Ferrari 246s, its only real competition.

For 1959, Cooper added the New Zealand driver Bruce McLaren and the American Masten Gregory to the team. Ferrari had Behra, Brooks and two more American drivers, Phil Hill and Dan Gurney. Both were Californians who had driven in sports-car races in the United States which were run on circuits like European road races. Cooper won eight of the 13 races they entered, taking the Constructors' title. Brabham took the Drivers' title.

The following year, 1960, was the last for the 2.5-litre formula. From 1961, cubic capacity would be limited to 1.5 litres with the option of using a 500-cc supercharged engine. Car makers were making plans for the new formula so it was a transitional year. Ferrari had tried a mid-engined 2.5-litre car which was unsuccessful, but for 1960 he had a mid-engined Formula Two car, the 1.5-litre Type 156, ready and it was raced in some World Championship events. He fielded the 246s with a strong team which now included the German driver Wolfgang von Trips.

The car which stole the headlines that year was the Type 18 Lotus. Chapman had contested the 1959 season with front-engined Lotus 16s driven by Graham Hill and Innes Ireland. For 1960, he abandoned the front-engine and followed and improved on the Cooper layout. Chapman went in pursuit of lightness: the body was fibreglass and the rear suspension was of a radical, lighter design. The car was very low on the ground and its power-to-weight ratio, expressed in bhp per tonne, was a long way ahead of its rivals: the Ferrari had 500 bhp per tonne, and the Cooper 530; the Lotus had 630.

Its first Grand Prix was in Argentina. Innes Ireland came sixth – a good result considering the car had only been finished a few days before the race. Rob Walker bought a Lotus 18 for Stirling Moss who won the Monaco Grand Prix in it.

At the British Grand Prix, the grid showed how far British cars had come in a short time. The front row consisted of the two Coopers of Brabham and McLaren and the two mid-engined BRMs of Graham Hill and Jo Bonnier; in the second row there was Ireland's Lotus 18 and Gurney's BRM, then the first of only two Ferraris, driven by von Trips. The next row had two more Lotuses driven by Jim Clark, a young Scot, and John Surtees, the former World Motor Cycle Champion; then there was Brooks in another Cooper and Phil Hill in the other Ferrari. The result was equally impressive: Brabham (Cooper), Surtees (Lotus), Ireland (Lotus), McLaren (Cooper) and Brooks (Lotus). The mid-engined car had arrived.

Front-engined cars had one last moment of glory at the Italian Grand Prix. The organizers included the banked oval in the race that year; it was fast but it was very bumpy and the British car makers and drivers decided that it was too dangerous. It was a walk-over for Ferrari: Phil Hill won in a Dino 246 with another American, Richie Ginther, second in another. Ferrari used the race to prepare for the following season; in fifth place was a mid-engined 156 driven by von Trips – Ferrari had finally put the horse behind the cart.

The British teams were not as well prepared for the new formula of 1961. Phil Hill won the World Championship, though sadly only after his teammate, von Trips, was killed while in a leading position. In 1962, supporters of BRM were finally rewarded for the years of investment when Graham Hill won the World Championship.

But Ferrari and BRM could not stop the steady advance of Chapman and Lotus. In 1962, Chapman brought out another completely new design, this time one which was to have far-reaching effects on the design of all racing cars: the Lotus 25, the first modern racing car with a monocoque. A monocoque is a 'single shell', dispensing with internal frames and relying on the inherent strength of the body itself, which in the Lotus 25 was made of fibreglass. The Lotus 25 had a new 1.5-litre, fuel-injected Coventry-Climax engine which gave around 200 bhp neatly enclosed in the body. Like other epochal cars before it, it was both functional and beautiful.

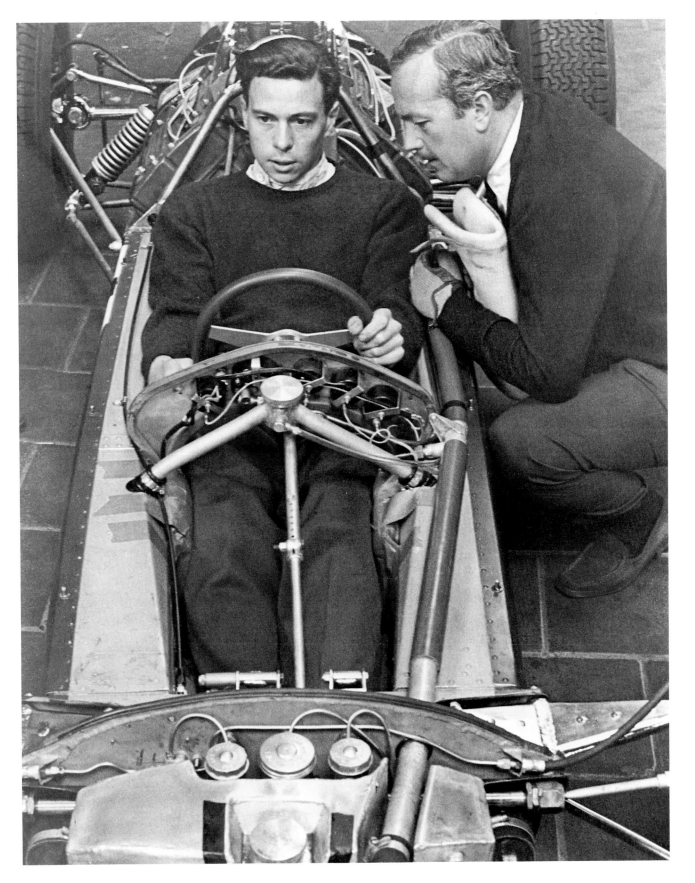

PAGE 155 Jim Clark and Colin Chapman with the revolutionary, monocoque Lotus 25 in 1962. Their relationship was a very close one and its strength contributed to the success of Lotus during the 1960s.

LEFT Clark and Chapman at Indianapolis in 1965, enjoying a great moment in their lives. Clark was killed in a Formula Two race at Hockenheim in Germany in 1968; Chapman continued to be the innovative genius and ruthless businessman at Lotus, and played a major part in transforming the sport before he died of a heart attack in 1982.

BELOW Clark in the Lotus 38 at Indianapolis in 1965, the year he became the first European driver for 45 years to win the American classic.

Chapman then matched the new car with the new driving star, Jim Clark, with whom he built up a close personal relationship. In 1963, Clark won seven of the ten events in the World Championship to win both titles.

Even before winning their first World Championship, Chapman was looking across the Atlantic to the financially rewarding American classic, the Indianapolis 500. Only a small number of European drivers had taken part in the race during its time as a World Championship event, and it lost that status in 1960. Grand Prix racing had been

ABOVE Classic Lotuses: the Lotus 18 (foreground), Colin Chapman's first rear-engined car, and the Lotus 25 monocoque.

RIGHT Classic engine of the 1.5-litre Formula: the V-8 Coventry-Climax which powered the Lotus 25. The Climax series of racing engines originated in 1953; the ready availability of high-quality components such as these engines was one of the key factors enabling Britain to develop its highly successful racing car business.

inaugurated in the United States in 1959 and McLaren, driving a Cooper, won the first race, held on a disused airfield at Sebring in Florida.

Gurney had seen the Lotus 25 at the Dutch Grand Prix at Zandvoort in 1962, and approached Chapman with the idea of taking on the American racing establishment, and what now looked to be the increasingly obsolete roadster cars, at Indianapolis. This was the first serious challenge by Europeans to Americans on American home ground since the early 1920s. Gurney took Chapman to the event, then arranged a meeting with the Ford Motor Company who were considering getting into the sport as part of its 'Total Performance' programme aimed at improving the image of its cars to a younger generation.

Ford toyed with backing Lotus or the American chassis designer, Watson, who had produced the last four Indianapolis winners. In the end, because of Clark's World Championship record and a demonstration by Clark at Indianapolis, Ford decided to go with Lotus. Chapman designed a new car,

the Lotus 29, around a 4.2-litre Ford engine which was to go into the Fairlane passenger car. The engine produced 370 bhp, but was also very efficient and the Lotus 29 would require one less pit stop for fuel than the traditional Indianapolis cars.

Two Lotus 29s were produced for the 1963 Indianapolis, one for Clark and one for Gurney. Clark was fifth fastest in practice. Parnelli Jones in his Agajanian-Willard Battery Special was fastest at just over 150 mph. At the start Jones went into the lead and, knowing that he would have to make an extra stop for fuel, tried to build up a big margin over Clark and Gurney. The roadsters came in for their first pit stop after 62 laps and Clark and Gurney went into first and second place. When Jones rejoined, he was 17 seconds behind Gurney.

On the 95th lap, Clark made his first pit stop and came out 40 seconds behind Jones; Gurney was even further behind after a bad stop. Jones made his second pit stop in 21 seconds while yellow cautionary lights were on, obliging drivers to hold their positions. He rejoined in the lead by 11 seconds. Clark steadily eroded the lead until by lap 175 it was down to 5 seconds. Then Jones started leaking oil: there were heated debates between the team managers and race officials and binoculars were trained on Jones' car but, rightly or wrongly, he was not called in and went on to win the race. It was a fortunate victory, but the mid-engined cars had clearly given the roadster designers something to think about.

Chapman and Clark came back the following year with the Lotus 34, but sadly their tyres were not up to the track. They lost their treads and A. J. Foyt won. It was the last time a front-engined car won at Indianapolis. For 1965, there were two Lotuses on the front row of the grid: Clark in the latest 38 and Foyt in one of the previous year's 34s. Foyt led at the start, but Clark overtook him on lap three. He never lost the lead again except during pit stops and won the race and a substantial cash prize for Lotus: $150,000.

The technical revolution was over, but Chapman would go on to make other changes in the sport which would have far-reaching consequences.

TOP Rookie year: A. J. Foyt in the Dean Van Lines Special at Indianapolis in 1958; he came 16th.

ABOVE Winner's circle: Foyt celebrating his first victory in 1961; his speed was 139.130 mph.

A.J. FOYT JR

Over 30 years of racing, A. J. Foyt can truly be described as a motor racing legend. He has won the Indianapolis 500 four times, one of only three drivers to do so. (The others are Al Unser Sr and Rick Mears.) He has been United States National Champion a record seven times. His first victory at Indianapolis, in 1961, came amid high drama on the track: while leading the race by ten seconds from Eddie Sachs, he was called into the pits for an extra stop because the refuelling system had not put enough in previously. Sachs went into a commanding lead, but with three laps to go, the tread of one of his tyres came off; he had to go into the pits giving victory to Foyt.

BELOW **Double first: in 1967, Foyt won Indianapolis for the third time in a Ford-engined car of his own construction. The same year, he won the 24-hour race at Le Mans in a Ford GT40 with Dan Gurney.**

ABOVE **Still racing: born in 1935, Foyt had made 31 consecutive starts at Indianapolis by 1988.**

CHAPTER SIX
RACING FOR ALL

Motor racing has brought about a great many improvements in the motor car, but the technical gulf between racing cars at the top level – Grands Prix in Europe and the Indianapolis 500 in the United States – and the cars we drive on the road, has steadily widened throughout the history of the sport. A racing car is, by definition, 'state of the art' technology, an embodiment of the latest, experimental ideas in design and engineering. Like a thoroughbred horse, it needs constant, skilled attention. Even with such care, it is temperamental, breaking down frequently. But it only has to sustain its peak performance for a few hours to achieve its purpose – to win on a well-known circuit, over a relatively short distance.

On the other hand, the essence of a modern family saloon car is endurance, reliability and the ability to cope with the unexpected. We expect the cars we drive to sustain their performance over thousands of miles, in all manner of different weather conditions and over different surfaces, with hundreds of stops and starts. Since the Second World War, competitive events for sports and saloon cars have grown in number and toughness; variations of the cars we see on the roads every day are raced and rallied to their limits, the most successful entries coming from manufacturers who spend huge sums supporting works teams. The reason is the same as it has been since the beginning of motor racing: winning races, and the aura of performance which goes with it, sells cars.

RIGHT **From Paris across the Sahara Desert to Dakar, capital of Senegal, West Africa, in 20 days: Bjorn Waldegard driving a Peugeot 405 in 1990 in the most famous long-distance rally. He came second. The winner was Ari Vatanen in a similar car.**

The main characteristic of races for sports and saloon cars is endurance. The best-known event is the Le Mans 24-hour race for sports cars which was first held in 1923, but there are many others whose names also reflect the keynote of endurance: the gruelling 24-hour race for saloon cars at Spa Francorchamps in Belgium, the 12-hour events at Sebring in Florida and the 1000 kilometre race at the Nürburgring for sports cars. Rallies have even tougher sounding names: the 1000 Lakes in Finland, the London to Sydney, the Paris to Dakar.

Car ownership has grown massively since the war, and with that growth has come a rich diversity of events which provide thrilling entertainment for spectators, many of whom will stay up all night at Le Mans or struggle up mountainsides to see the rally cars go by. But the ultimate purpose of such events is to demonstrate the reliability of cars to those spectators who are also potential customers. To compete successfully manufacturers' cars must be seen in competitions – and they must win.

After the war, organizers of the established endurance events were eager to start them up again. Some races came back only to disappear; others were modified to suit the post-war era; and some would thrive alongside a whole host of new events. The Le Mans circuit had been taken over by the *Luftwaffe* during the war and used as an airfield. It had been severely damaged, but in 1949 was once again ready for the 24-hour race. One of the oldest events, the Targa Florio, first run in 1906, was restarted in 1948. The Monte Carlo Rally, first run in 1911, re-emerged in 1949 after a 10-year break; the cars still started from cities all over Europe and the rally retained its link with the luxury sports car market of a more elegant age with a '*Concours de Confort*', a competition for the most comfortable car. But the first of these great events to restart after the war was the Mille Miglia.

The Italian classic had nearly been cancelled forever in 1938 when ten people, including seven children, were killed in a crash. But it was a wonderful showcase for the Italian motor industry – millions of people turned out along the route which took in most of the major towns in northern Italy – and in 1947 it was revived. It was an all-Italian race, since in post-war Europe few manufacturers or individuals from other countries had the money to travel as far as Italy. The great Italian companies made the best of it: some ran works-backed teams while others, including Alfa which was short of funds and already supporting a Grand Prix team, relied on private individuals, many driving pre-war cars. Clemente Biondetti and Emilio Romano had a pre-war 2.9-litre Alfa, though they had to remove its superchargers to comply with new regulations. Other major companies took on the top drivers: Piero Taruffi and Tazio Nuvolari, now 55 and a sick man, were driving for a new Italian company, Cisitalia, and Luigi Villoresi was driving a Maserati. But the great majority of the 155 entries in 1947 were amateurs, private individuals with a racing licence who simply wanted the thrill of taking part – many drove saloon cars, nearly a third drove 1100 cc Fiat sports cars.

The race proper was betwen Nuvolari (who had a co-driver but characteristically did all the driving himself) and Biondetti and Romano in their Alfa. Nuvolari was leading by up to 9 minutes for much of the first half of the race, then the weather broke bringing torrential rain. The Cisitalia was an open sports car and he was soon drenched to the skin, but he raced on until water caused electrical problems. Biondetti and Romano, snug in their closed Alfa, took over the lead. Once he was moving again, Nuvolari drove like a man possessed, slowly gaining on the Alfa. But there was not enough time: he finished second, 16 minutes behind Biondetti and Romano.

For the following year's Mille Miglia, Biondetti and Nuvolari were both engaged by Enzo Ferrari to drive his new sports car, the Type 166. Ferrari was set on becoming a major manufacturer of sports cars, and moved into racing them as vigorously as he had moved into Grands Prix. The open-topped Type 166 had a 2-litre, V-12 engine giving around 150 bhp. Nuvolari and Biondetti were both driving 166s, yet Nuvolari managed to build up an incredible 29-minute lead over his teammate. In doing so, he nearly wrecked the car, losing a mudguard here, the bonnet there. When the driver's seat came adrift from its moorings, he stopped and replaced it with a sack of oranges. He was now a sick man, coughing and spitting blood, and he knew he was slowly dying. But his indomitable competitive spirit triumphed over his wasted body in what he must have known was his last chance to win the Mille Miglia again. Seeing him during a stop at Maranello, Ferrari tried, but failed, to get him to retire. There were darkly whispered stories of a wish to die at the wheel of a racing car in a race. His driving skill had not deserted him but his luck ran out: near Parma, the Ferrari's brakes failed and he stopped by the side of the road. A priest found him, exhausted, still in the car, lifted him out and put him to bed. Biondetti won for Ferrari, but the 1948 Mille Miglia will always be remembered for Nuvolari's epic drive and personal anguish. If he had wanted to die at the wheel, he was to be disappointed: he died, in bed, in 1953 and was mourned throughout Italy.

The Mille Miglia was changing. Despite the obvious hazards of the race, the organizers went on encouraging the widest possible range of drivers and cars, including a class for touring models introduced in 1949. The response was huge: the entry list nearly doubled from 167 starters in 1948 to 303

in 1949; by 1950 it had risen to 375, and by 1952 it had reached 501. It still attracted the top works teams with the top drivers, but the vast majority of the cars were ordinary family saloons such as Fiat Topolinos – saloon cars, specially prepared by their owners at home.

The idea of racing ordinary, or 'stock', cars had taken root in America before the war. Essentially showroom models modified for racing, they were first raced on an organized basis during the 1930s. It is part of American racing folklore that many of these 'hotted up' cars originated during the Prohibition era, specially built by bootleggers to carry moonshine whisky from state to state in hidden tanks. They looked like ordinary cars, but under the bonnet they had been tinkered with by expert mechanics to make them that little bit faster than similar cars driven by the police and excise men.

The place most associated with stock-car racing in the south-eastern United States is Ormond Beach at Daytona in Florida, where the sand was excep-

North Curve, Daytona Beach 1936: the 250-mile race was stopped after 200 miles because the surface had been churned up so badly. Milt Marion, leading in a Ford, was the winner at an average speed of 48.94 mph.

tionally hard-packed. Ever since 1902, people who wanted to drive their cars fast, including at one time Henry Ford who was a great devotee of the idea that speed sold cars, had come to Daytona. During the 1920s and 1930s, many Land Speed record attempts were made on the beach, but once speeds started approaching 300 mph, drivers moved to the Bonneville Salt Flats in Utah where they had more space. The attempts had always been good for business in Daytona and in 1936, after they had moved to Utah, the Chamber of Commerce promoted a race for stock cars to replace the spectacle. It was over 250 miles, round a 3.2-mile circuit which was laid out over a section of the beach and a parallel section of road behind it, linked by a turn at either end. There were 28 entries, most of them Fords, competing for a prize of $5000.

Although thousands of spectators turned out along the dunes to watch, not all of them paid for their tickets and the event was not a financial success. But the race itself was an exciting, if rather amateur, spectacle: many cars got stuck in the sand on the turns and the tide came in before it was completely over. Even then, because of a complicated system of penalties, the result was not announced for several days. Fords filled the first five places. The winner was Milt Marion and in fifth place was the man who had prepared the winning car: his mechanic Bill France, who had driven in the race in a borrowed 1935 Ford.

France was a man of vision and an entrepreneur. He saw a great future for stock-car racing if only it could be properly organized. The early races at Daytona were run on an *ad hoc* basis, but after the Second World War he set about putting them on a proper footing. He approached the American Automobile Association (AAA), hoping for assistance in setting up an official structure, but was brushed aside: stock-car racing was not their priority. Undaunted, he brought together the leading drivers and promoters in the developing sport and, in a smoke-filled room at the Streamline Hotel, Daytona, on 12 December 1947, he made a speech which prophesied a great future for stock-car racing, a period of great expansion. He argued

that if they organized the sport properly, promoting stock-car races could become a financially successful enterprise. Soon afterwards, the National Association for Stock Car Auto Racing (NASCAR) was formed and France was elected president.

The first race organized by NASCAR took place at Daytona Beach on 14 February 1948, on a road-and-beach circuit similar to the one used before the war. The drivers had an unofficial race to the event, meeting up at points across the south-eastern states, then racing to Daytona; the unofficial winning post was France's petrol station. Thirty-two cars started the official race and 12 finished; the winner was Bob 'Red' Byron driving a 1939 Ford. The drivers became local heroes, stars even, and to prevent them being lured away to events sanctioned by other bodies, France made sure they were contractually bound to NASCAR.

France gained a solid reputation for promoting good racing and, before long, NASCAR was being asked to organize races further afield. It eventually became a private corporation with France at its head and proved to be the financial success he had always believed possible. In the first year, NASCAR held 85 races; in the second, 394. At the victory dinner in 1949, the association distributed $64,000 to drivers; by 1951, the prize money was over $750,000. On Labor Day 1950, NASCAR held its first 500-mile race at Darlington Beach, South Carolina – Indianapolis had a challenger.

France and his drivers went on racing throughout the 1950s, and stock-car racing grew in popularity. But development around Ormond Beach was encroaching on the area where races were held and the track had to be moved each year. What was needed was a permanent site. As early as 1955, France had formed the Daytona Beach Motor Speedway Corporation with a view to building a track between a dog track and the airport.

He announced that he would build the speedway in time to hold the first race, the Daytona 500 for 'late model stock cars', on George Washington's birthday – 22 February – in 1959. He borrowed money, then sold tickets in advance to keep up the payments. The track was built, and the race went ahead as planned. There were 59 entries and Cotton

Owens was fastest in practice at 143 mph in a 1958 Pontiac. Once under way, the event settled down in the early stages to a three-way battle between Bob Welborn in a Chevrolet, Joe Weatherly in another and Tom Pistones in a Plymouth. Then a local driver, Glenn 'Fireball' Roberts, a veteran of the beach-racing days, came through in a Pontiac. Lee Petty then joined the leaders in his Oldsmobile, followed by Johnny Beauchamp in a Ford Thunderbird.

The lead was constantly changing, which delighted the crowd. One reason was a phenomenon which the drivers only discovered during the race – what they were later to call 'drafting'. The circuit was 2½ miles long on a tri-oval design, that is, there were three corners and three straights. Each of the corners was steeply banked, at 31 degrees. As the drivers came out of the corners, they noticed that they could sometimes overtake their rivals with ease, while at other times they were effortlessly passed. The car behind was getting a tow from the slipstream of the car in front. Drafting quickly developed as a tactic. Round the banked curves, drivers held a position right behind the car in front. Then, as they came out of the curve, they used the extra speed the tow gave them to overtake. On the 200th lap, Petty and Beauchamp were virtually neck and neck, with a third car a lap behind. The three crossed the line together. Beauchamp was judged

to be the winner and was awarded the trophy. After three days of deliberation, France and the officials decided that the winner was Petty, by a hair's breadth, and there was another award ceremony.

ABOVE North Curve, Daytona Beach 1955: Glen 'Fireball' Roberts taking the famous corner in his Buick. The beach surface had been greatly improved after the war and speeds had risen. Tim Flock won the race at an average speed of 92.05 mph.

BELOW Daytona Speedway 1959: Lee Petty leading the pack on the new banked oval circuit which made the beach redundant. He won the inaugural race at an average speed of 135.52 mph.

RIGHT ABOVE **Early days: Don Garlitz, champion driver, in 1957.**

RIGHT BELOW **Funny Car: World Champion driver Bruce Larson** in 1990.

ABOVE **Top fuel car: Lori Johns, one of a small number of women** drivers, in 1990; 'fuel' is slang for nitro-methanol, which such dragsters use.

While Daytona was developing stock-car events in Florida, another type of racing, more loosely based on stock cars, was taking shape on the West Coast of America. California was a boom state in the post-war years and a new generation of young people grew up with money in their pockets. There were plenty of cars around and, for some young-sters with a mechanical interest, hotting up family saloons to race them against each other became the cool thing to do. The first competitions were highly unofficial – in fact, illegal. Two T-shirted young-sters met up on a public road, often in the middle of the night, and raced each other over a stretch of the public highway. The cars were built for acceleration and racing took the form of high-speed sprints. Drag racing had been born.

Dragsters took many forms, from a vehicle that looked like a rather fierce family car to a torpedo-shaped monster built from the drop fuel tanks discarded by United States Air Force fighters, with a stock engine mounted in the middle and a wheel at each corner. Races moved from roads to dried-

up lake beds in the desert where they took the form of a quarter-mile dash by two cars side by side. In the early days, it was a sport organized by and for the benefit of the participants; when they were not racing, they were watching or timekeeping. But the spectacle of outlandish cars hurtling down a strip in pairs, exhausts bellowing, clearly had commercial potential. In 1950, drag racing came of age when the first ticket event was held on the runways at Orange County airport, near Los Angeles in southern California.

The following year, the National Hot Rod Association (NHRA) was formed to establish rules for the new sport and Wally Parkes, the editor of *Hot Rod Magazine*, was elected its first president.

Drag racing expanded throughout the 1950s with commercial drag strips being built in other parts of the country. It developed its own technology and language. The classic, long, thin dragsters with their tiny front wheels and massive rear ones became known as 'rails'. The engine was known as the 'mill', and improving its performance to the limit, with multiple banks of carburettors and superchargers, without blowing it up became an intricate science. Transforming that power into acceleration, rather than a cloud of smoking rubber, was just as important. New types of clutches were developed; tyres, known as 'slicks', became wider and new rubber compounds were used to make them stickier. Discarded drop tanks gave way to specially built, aerodynamically shaped, aluminium bodies; rear axles were narrowed to give the car a smaller frontal area and therefore less wind resistance; parachutes were used to slow dragsters down after a run.

Performance steadily improved. In 1958, a rail with a supercharged Oldsmobile engine covered the quarter-mile in 10.1 seconds; by 1962, Tommy 'TV' Ivo had reduced the time to 8 seconds. In 1967, Don Prudhomme was the first under 7 seconds, 6.99 seconds. By 1975, Don Garlitz had it down to 5.63 seconds. The terminal speed of dragsters increased at the same time: in 1958, it was 157 mph; in 1966, Don Westerdale managed 210.76 mph; and in 1975 Garlitz took the speed to 250 mph.

From the late 1960s, a new breed of dragster started to become popular. 'Funny Cars' were strange, elongated versions of production family cars, their bodywork distorted to fit over a dragster chassis and engine. These replica road cars were beautifully turned out, hand-finished icons of the cult of speed, and steadily began to take over in popularity from the rails. The key to their success was that their shape was similar to that of cars which spectators could buy. Design began to come full circle as manufacturers incorporated the styling of the Funny Cars into their production models.

Road racing had never been the tradition in the United States. The democratic principles of American law made it difficult for promoters to get public roads closed for racing, while the spirit of free enterprise was invoked to keep events in places where spectators could be charged for entry. But American and European sports cars were popular with collectors in the United States and, in 1944, the Sports Car Club of America (SCCA) was formed to preserve the cars and organize events where enthusiasts could congregate. Gradually the SSCA was drawn into organizing sports-car races. World-class American road-racing drivers such as Phil Hill, Dan Gurney and Richie Ginther learnt their skills at SCCA events on circuits like the one built on a disused airfield at Sebring in Florida.

Road racing on the heroic scale of the Mille Miglia and the Targa Florio had never flourished in America, but in 1950 a superb race for production cars was run in Mexico: the Carrera Panamericana. The Mexican section of the Pan American Highway, a road planned eventually to link Alaska to Cape Horn, was finished that year and, to celebrate, the Mexican government organized a 3000 km race along it between 5 May and 11 May.

THE CARRERA PANAMERICANA

BELOW The start: Tuxtla Gutiérrez near the Guatemalan border, 1952.

RIGHT ABOVE The race: around Mexico City crowd control was good, but in the country areas it was frequently non-existent.

RIGHT BELOW The finish: the winner of the saloon-car class in the 1952 race, a Lincoln driven by Walt Faulkner, at Ciudad Juárez on the United States–Mexico border.

American drivers responded with relish; there were 132 entries and 58 finished. The winner was Herschel McGriff driving a 1950 Oldsmobile 88, the fastest saloon car at that time.

The Carrera quickly established itself as an important event in the racing calendar and manufacturers in Europe were eager to see their cars participate in such an effective shop window for the huge American car market. In 1951, there were separate classes for saloon cars and sports cars and European drivers, schooled in the road-racing tradition, soon established themselves in the sports-car class. A Ferrari Inter, a derivative of the Type 166, driven by Taruffi with Luigi Chinetti, won; another, driven by Alberto Ascari, came second.

But the jewel in the crown of sports-car racing, the showcase which all sports-car enthusiasts, and consequently manufacturers, looked to has always been the Le Mans 24-hour race. It started as an event for touring cars, and the original regulations stated that entries had to have four seats, that they should appear in the company's catalogue and that a minimum of 30 road-going examples had to be built. This process, known as 'homologation', was designed to prevent manufacturers building one-off special cars which were not available to paying customers. But even before the Second World War, there had been a move towards a more specialized form of racing sports car with two seats. In 1949, to broaden the base for entries in the lean years after the war, the Auto Club d'Ouest (ACO), which organized the race, permitted what it called 'prototype' sports cars. There were built in tiny numbers, simply to race, and were not destined for the showrooms; their success simply added lustre to the name of their road-going cousins.

The Ferrari Type 166, in which Biondetti had won both the Mille Miglia and the Targa Florio in 1948, repeating the double in 1949, put the Ferrari name firmly on the sports-car map. In the line-up for the first post-war Le Mans, two T166s were running against 29 assorted, large French sports cars, and 16 British cars including a Bentley which the French importer of the marque thought would be good publicity. Chinetti, partnered briefly by Lord Selsdon who was taken ill and only drove for two hours of the race, won in a Ferrari. Having won the Mille Miglia, Targa Florio and Le Mans 24-hour race all in the same year, Ferrari was rapidly establishing itself as a major force in sports-car racing as well as in Grands Prix.

But Ferrari's place in the limelight at Le Mans was short-lived. In 1950, Talbot took its 4.5-litre Grand Prix cars, fitted them with a wider body, a two-seat cockpit, mudguards and lights to conform with the regulations, and raced them as sports cars. One was driven at Le Mans that year by the Frenchman Louis Rosier, partnered by his son. All the Ferraris retired, leaving the Talbots to take a popular first and second. The winner was Rosier, who was at the wheel for over 23 of the 24 hours.

But his victory did not signal a French revival. Behind the Talbots came a string of British cars: an Allard, driven by Sydney Allard and Tom Cole, an Austin Healey driven by Tony Rolt and Duncan Hamilton, then an Aston Martin driven by George Abecassis and Lance Macklin. In 12th and 15th places were two modified Jaguar XK120 sports cars which had put up some of the fastest lap times: Jaguar went home knowing that they had a car fast enough to win. With echoes of the string of successes by Bentley 20 years previously, it was the British, in particular Jaguar, who were on the march at Le Mans.

The Jaguars had been privately entered, with technical support overseen by a Jaguar engineer, 'Lofty' England. Back in Coventry, finance was found to uprate the XK120 still further. The new car was the C Type and, for 1951, the company entered a works team of three cars and six drivers: Stirling Moss with Jack Fairman; Peter Whitehead and Peter Walker; and the ex-Ferrari driver, Biondetti partnered by Leslie Johnson. Moss started well down the start line, but went into an early lead; after the first two hours he had lapped all the other entries. At one point, the Jaguars were in first, second and third places but the Moss and Fairman and Biondetti and Johnson cars had to retire with oil-pressure problems. Whitehead and Walker managed to stay to the end, winning from Talbot and Aston Martin. It was the beginning of a long love affair between Jaguar and Le Mans.

The 1951 race also saw the first appearance of a new name which was to be even more directly associated than Jaguar with sports-car racing, and particularly with Le Mans: Porsche. Way down the overall placings, in 20th place, but winning the 751–1100 cc class, was the small Porsche 356. It was driven by Auguste Veuillet, the Porsche distributor in France, and its class victory had an instant effect on sales. Dr Ferry Porsche, son of the great designer of the Volkswagen and the pre-war Auto Union Grand Prix cars, had a policy of promoting his cars through racing in preference to taking space in newspapers; he found that victories, and the editorial which went with them, were more effective. The company incorporated the names of

great races into the names of its cars: after a Porsche 356, driven by Prince Metternich, came eighth overall in the Carrera Panamericana, the suffix Carrera was used for derivatives of the 356 and on later models, particularly the 911.

In 1952, Mercedes-Benz returned to motor racing, competing in selected sports-car races, including Le Mans. Its car was the 150-mph 300 SL with distinctive 'gull-wing' doors which opened upwards. Mercedes had a formidable reputation in motor racing, built on its success before the First World War and in the 1930s. Jaguar, fearful of their speed, had modified the shape of the C Types to make them even faster. But in doing so, it also

Two Porsche 356s from the company's own collection on its famous test track at Weissach, Germany.

altered the cooling system with disastrous results: all three Jaguars overheated during the race and had to pull out. There were several Ferraris in the race, one driven by Ascari, but only one managed to stay the whole 24 hours, and it was not fast enough to beat the Mercedes driven by Hermann Lang and Fritz Riess. Mercedes' foray into sports-car racing in 1952 was a great success: they won four events, including the top two – Le Mans and the Carrera Pan-americana – with Karl Kling at the wheel.

THE PORSCHE FAMILY CAR

Ferry Porsche was born in 1909 at Wiener-Neustadt in Austria where his father, Dr Ferdinand Porsche, was technical director of the Austro-Daimler company. His childhood was spent in daily contact with the world of innovative engineering which his father created. Early on, the young Porsche was exposed to skilled workers in the Daimler factory from whom he absorbed a love for, and detailed knowledge of, motor cars and how they worked. In the 1930s, he worked on, and drove, the mid-engined Auto Union Grand Prix cars. When his father established his independent Porsche design office, Ferry worked on the design of the original Volkswagen. The VW was adapted for military purposes during the Second World War and, in the chaos of post-war Austria, father and son were imprisoned by the French. In 1947, they started to pick up the threads of their motor-car business once again.

They had always wanted to build a sports car based on Volkswagen parts and, once the Volkswagen factory was in production again, they began work on one: the Porsche 356. The first car to bear the family name was built from second-hand parts and completed on 8 June 1948, achieving 80 mph in tests in the Katchberg Pass. A month later the 356, driven by Ferry Porsche's cousin Herbert Kaes, won a road race near Innsbruck: a dynasty of sports cars had been born.

RIGHT **Dr Ferry Porsche** in 1984.

ABOVE The start of a motoring legend: the Porsche 356. The Porsche theme of good design was carried throughout the car and accessories.

LEFT AND BELOW Vindication at Le Mans: the Porsche 356 at the 1951 Le Mans 24-hour race in which Auguste Veuillet and Edmond Mouche won the 751–1100 cc class and finished twentieth overall.

Jaguar was back on top at Le Mans in 1953 though its cars were not the fastest in the race. The firm's advantage that year was that instead of drum brakes, it had fitted disc brakes which were much more effective, enabling drivers to brake later at each corner. The event was a triumph for Jaguar who took three of the first four places. First went to Rolt and Hamilton, second to Moss and Walker. An American sports car – a Cunningham – was third, with another Jaguar fourth.

In 1953, a World Championship was introduced for sports-car manufacturers, another tool in the battle for the eye of the public. It covered seven races: Spa-Francorchamps, the Mille Miglia, the 1000 km at the Nürburgring, Sebring, Le Mans, the Tourist Trophy at Dundrod in Northern Ireland and the Carrera Panamericana. Giannino Marzotto won the Mille Miglia, Giuseppe Farina and Mike Hawthorn the 1000 km at Spa, Ascari the 1000 km at the Nürburgring, all for Ferrari, and the company did well enough in the other events to take the title in its first year, adding a little more sparkle to the Ferrari name.

The 1954 Le Mans was a battle between Ferrari and Jaguar. Speeds were rising and both companies had brought out new cars: Jaguar the sleeker D Type and Ferrari the 375MM, both capable of around 170 mph. Ferrari had taken on José Froilan Gonzalez, Maurice Trintignant, Umberto Maglioli, Marzotto, Rosier and Robert Manzon. The Jaguars, one of which was driven by Moss, were better than the Ferraris in the rainy conditions, but Moss retired and Gonzalez and Trintignant won.

Ferrari won the Sports Car World Championship again in 1954. In addition to Le Mans, Farina and Maglioli won the 1000 km race in Buenos Aires in a 375, with Harry Schell and Alfonso de Portago second in another; Marzotto was second in the Mille Miglia behind Ascari in a Lancia; and Maglioli won the last Carrera Panamericana for Ferrari driving a 375, with Phil Hill second in another. The Carrera was cancelled after the 1954 race because of the high level of accidents. It had also become too costly and inconvenient to close an important road so that European and American car makers could show off their wares.

JAGUAR'S FINEST 24 HOURS

In 1953, Ferrari won its sixth Mille Miglia in a row; Jaguar entered the race but made no impression. Ferrari's challenger for Le Mans that year was the 375MM. At 320 bhp, it was 100 bhp more than the Jaguar, but, with its sleeker body, the C Type was only 1 mph slower. Stirling Moss went into an early lead for Jaguar, but had to stop with fuel problems. By the time he got going again, he was back in 21st place. Meanwhil another Jaguar, driven by Tony Rolt and Duncan Hamilton, battled it out with Luigi Villoresi and Albert Ascari in the 375MM, the Jaguar drivers gradually building up a two-lap lead. Moss and Peter Walker managed to claw their way back to third place overnight Around 10.30 on the Sunday morning, the 375 retired with a slipping clutch, leaving Jaguars in first and second places which they retained; a third Jaguar was fourth.

Following their other great year at Le Mans, 1957, when Jaguars filled the first four places, winning their fifth Le Mans in seven years, they were absent from racing and did not return until the late 1980s. Mercedes also returned to battle it out with its old rivals from the 1950s. Since then, Jaguar won in 1988, Mercedes in 198 and Jaguar again in 1990.

ABOVE **A great day for England, 27 June 1953: manager 'Lofty' England (left) with the winning pair of drivers, Tony Rolt (centre) and Duncan Hamilton (right), in the Jaguar pit at Le Mans.**

ABOVE RIGHT **The winning Jaguar C Type.**

OPPOSITE **Jaguar mechanics reading about their success in the French motor-racing press.**

In 1955, Mercedes brought out a new sports car, the 300SLR. Apart from the name, these cars had little to do with the 300SL, but were derived from the W196 Grand Prix car, with a 3-litre version of the straight eight engine. One of their first outings was the legendary Mille Miglia and Mercedes took its two top Grand Prix drivers, Juan Manuel Fangio and Moss to drive them.

There was an all-time record entry for the 1955 Mille Miglia: 521 cars. Not only was the entry getting bigger, it was also getting wider: bubble cars, 350 cc three-wheelers, had been introduced in 1954 and were back in 1955, now with a class to themselves. It was the only race in which a bubble car could compete against 310 bhp pure-bred sports cars modelled on the latest German Grand Prix cars and capable of 185 mph.

Second drivers were no longer mandatory and Fangio chose to drive alone, looking more like a Grand Prix entrant in his single seat. Moss, on the other hand, decided to take a navigator, Denis Jenkinson, rather than a co-driver. It was a wise move. Moss did not know the route as well as many of the Italian drivers did, so he and Jenkinson went over it minutely before the race, making pace notes for every corner, every straight, noting speeds, distances, gears. It was a highly professional approach with a special system of hand signals which Jenkinson used during the race to convey information to Moss; each had to trust the other completely. They covered the 998 miles in 10 hours, 7 minutes and 48 seconds – to win by 32 minutes from Fangio in the other 300SLR, Moss's average speed of 98.3 mph broke the existing record by nearly 10 mph.

With the record entry and Moss's superb drive, 1955 marked the high point of the Mille Miglia. It was surprising that it had lasted as long as it had. With over 500 cars, of very different types, many of them driven by amateurs, on public roads, a serious accident was bound to happen. Ferrari swept the board in 1956, taking the first five places, and took the first three the following year. But 1957 was the last race. The Mille Miglia was cancelled forever following the death of Alfonso de Portago, his co-driver and ten spectators.

THE LAST YEARS OF THE MILLE MIGLIA

In 1954 drivers were allowed in the Mille Miglia without a co-driver. Like many of the top drivers, Alberto Ascari chose to drive alone, winning the race for Lancia in a D24 at an average speed of 87.3 mph. A measure of the difference in the skill of the drivers in the race can be judged from the numbers on the side of the cars: Ascari, who left Brescia at 6.02 a.m., is about to pass a Fiat (ABOVE) which left at 19 minutes to midnight, over six hours previously.

In 1955, Stirling Moss (LEFT) became the first British driver to win the Mille Miglia. He was partnered by the motor racing journalist Denis Jenkinson as navigator in the Mercedes 300SLR, and their average speed of 98.5 mph has never been beaten. It was a famous victory commemorated in oils (RIGHT ABOVE) by the artist Frank Wootton.

In 1957 the motor racing photographer Louis Klemantaski sat alongside Peter Collins in the last Mille Miglia and recorded a vivid impression (RIGHT) of the view from the co-driver's seat.

When Mercedes took the 300SLR to Le Mans for the 1955 24-hour race it was obviously a great favourite. Its leading car was driven by the most talented driving partnership which could be put together: Fangio, the current Formula One World Champion, and Moss, whose recent victory in the Mille Miglia was still a talking point. Another 300SLR was driven by Pierre Levegh. Jaguar's leading driver Hawthorn, partnered by Ivor Bueb, drove a D Type. It promised to be a great race.

Eugenio Castellotti went into the lead at the start for Ferrari, but a duel between Fangio in the 300SLR and Hawthorn in the D Type gradually took them to the front. On the 42nd lap, at 6.30 pm, Hawthorn was heading for the pits. He had passed Macklin who was driving an Austin Healey in a smaller class. Macklin was doing 130 mph followed by Levegh who was, in turn, followed by Fangio. As Hawthorn pulled over, he touched the brakes and on came the brake lights; Macklin moved to avoid him and Levegh, travelling at 150 mph, hit him from behind. Levegh's Mercedes somersaulted over the safety barrier, caught fire and broke into pieces which flew into the crowd, killing a total of 83 people and injuring over 100. It was the worst accident in motor-racing history. The race continued, but once the full extent of the casualties became clear, Mercedes withdrew its team. Jaguar stayed and Hawthorn went on to win a sad and rather hollow victory.

BELOW AND RIGHT ABOVE **Motor racing's worst moment: Pierre Levegh's car somersaults into the crowd at Le Mans in 1955. He was 50 years old when he died; his wife was in the crowd which witnessed the accident. An American serviceman in France, Jimmy Prickett, from Texas, took these two photographs.**

RIGHT BELOW **The dead. It seems extraordinary now that a race in which over 80 people were killed and more than 100 injured went on for another 20 hours. One reason given for continuing the event was that cancelling it would have caused a mass exodus from the track, which would have hindered rescue operations and the care of the injured.**

ABOVE International Production Car race at Silverstone in 1962. The powerful road-going Jaguars were one of the favourites of the day, but the smaller Mini is already evident on the grid.

BELOW In Britain, saloon-car racing started after the Second World War and, by the 1960s, was an established part of the motor-racing calendar. Jim Clark was a great participant: by 1964, he was the World Champion in Formula One, but he still came to Brands Hatch in Kent that year to race the Lotus Cortina.

LEFT Brands Hatch started out as a motor-cycle grass track circuit in the 1930s. This aerial view shows the first British Grand Prix to be held on this circuit, in 1964. Clark won the race for Lotus.

In October 1955, Moss and Peter Collins won the Targa Florio in a 300SLR, but it was the end of Mercedes in racing. It won the Sports Car World Championship in 1955, but then pulled out. Racing had done its job for the firm: between 1954 and 1957 it sold 3258 300SLs, to a great extent on the back of the racing success associated with the 300SL and 300SLR. Today the 300SL remains one of the most collectable cars money can buy.

Britain dominated Le Mans for the rest of the decade, though Ferrari and Porsche were steadily advancing. In 1956, a privately entered Jaguar D Type driven by Ron Flockhart with Ninian Sanderson, and entered by Ecurie Ecosse, a Scottish-based private team, won the race after the Jaguar works cars had withdrawn or been damaged in crashes. In 1957, all the D Types were privately entered. It was a triumph: they filled the first four places, the first two going to Ecurie Ecosse.

In 1958, engine capacity was limited to 3 litres. The front runners were Aston Martin, and Ferrari with another new car: the 250 Testa Rossa. Phil Hill and Olivier Gendebien won for Ferrari with Aston second. Porsche was moving up the results table with third, fourth and fifth places overall and victory in the 1.5-litre class. In 1959, Aston Martin soundly beat the Ferraris, taking the first two places; Ferraris came third, fourth, fifth and sixth. Aston then withdrew, leaving Le Mans to the Italians.

There is a pattern to winning a Le Mans. A manufacturer makes a great effort and wins, sometimes several years in succession. Then a challenge comes from another firm which invests heavily enough to beat the previous winner who withdraws, or fades from the limelight for several years. Then along comes another challenger – and the cycle continues. From 1960, it was Ferrari's turn to shine at Le Mans: Paul Frère and Gendebien won in a Testa Rossa. In 1961, Ferrari won again with Gendebien partnered by Phil Hill. In that year, they had a new car in the race: the 246P, a mid-engined sports car with a V-6 engine. Enzo Ferrari, who had been reluctant to introduce the mid-engined layout in his Formula One cars, followed Porsche by introducing it into his sports cars.

ABOVE Paddy Hopkirk and his navigator at the 1964 Racing Car Show at Olympia after their Monte Carlo victory.

BELOW The ultimate Mini was the Mini-Cooper 'S': the car's association with Cooper, the Formula One car builders, further enhanced its fast, tough image.

RIGHT The Mini became a favourite with amateur rally drivers, further enhancing their image as different, spor[t] saloon cars. This in turn ma[de] them highly popular with customers, and they became one of Britain's most successf[ul] production cars since the Second World War.

BRITAIN'S INCREDIBLE MINIS

The Monte Carlo Rally had always had a rather traditional, sedate, very sporting image, with echoes of a bygone motoring age but, from 1961, it began to change into a more robust, commercial event. There were several factors: Anthony Noghes who had organized it since 1911 retired and was replaced by Monaco's greatest racing driver, Louis Chiron; special stages – fast stretches of road where speed counted for everything – were introduced for the first time; and works teams, with their professional drivers, practice runs, back-up vehicles, pace notes, ice notes for the mountain sections and their financial muscle, steadily began to take over from the private entrants.

The BMC Mini-Cooper arrived as the event was changing, and the British car contributed to the process. The first Mini appeared in the 1962 event, but for the next two years the Swedish driver Eric Carlsson won in his two-stroke Saab. In 1963, the British driver Paddy Hopkirk managed sixth place in a Mini then, in 1964, he won; Timo Mackinen won again for BMC in 1965. In 1966, Minis were initially placed first, second and third, but were disqualified because their lights were deemed to be at the wrong level. The decision caused a scandal, and there was more than a suggestion that the organizing committee simply could not bear the thought that the cheeky little car had won its prestigious event.

ABOVE AND LEFT **Ford GT40: one of the cars raced at Le Mans in 1965, where it was driven by Umberto Maglioli and Bob Bondurant. The colours date from 1968, when John Wyer uprated the cars and raced them with backing from Gulf Oil, winning in 1968 and 1969. In 1968, this GT40 came fourth in the 1000 km race at Spa-Francorchamps in Belgium, driven by David Hobbs and Paul Hawkins.**

With two victories in a row, Enzo Ferrari was on the march at Le Mans. Internationally, his firm had been highly successful. In the nine years up to 1961, he had taken the Sports Car World Championship title seven times; only Mercedes and Aston Martin broke his run, in 1955 and 1959. Ferrari's success made it prominent, especially in the United States, and this irked Ford, one of America's major manufacturers. Henry Ford II saw his Ford-backed, Ford-engined, AC Cobras beaten by Ferraris, at a time when the company was trying to woo the rich youth of the baby boom generation in America with its 'Total Performance Programme', a technical-cum-public-relations exercise that linked successful racing, in many areas of competition, to the marketing of Ford cars. Ferrari was stealing the limelight and Ford did not like it.

The American giant's first reaction was to try and buy the small Italian specialist builder, but the bid failed. Instead, Ford decided to build a car to beat Ferrari. Ford realized that, in taking on European manufacturers on their home territory, it would have to have European collaboration, and decided to build the car in Europe. To that

ABOVE AND OPPOSITE **Top of the range Ford GT40 Mk. II: one of the latest 7-litre models. This car was written off at Sebring in the United States in 1969, but has since been restored to peak condition.**

end, it formed a company, Ford Advanced Vehicles (FAV), to do the job. The FAV factory was established at Slough in Britain. Design studies started in May 1963 in America, using some features of the Ford Mustang sports car and the V-8, 4.2–litre engine from the Fairlane which was also being prepared with Lotus for their challenge at Indianapolis. Ford then engaged Eric Broadley of Lola to design the car. He had already built a promising sports car using the Fairlane engine.

While Ford worked on its challenge, Ferrari emphasized its complete dominance of Le Mans with a fourth straight victory in 1963, taking the first six places; an AC-Ford was in seventh place.

The Ford challenger was named the 'GT40', for Grand Touring and because it was 40 in. high. The first example was ready for testing in April 1964, and two made their first appearance at the Le Mans practice weekend that same month. It was not a good start: the cars were fast, but they were unpredictable at high speeds and both crashed. They were ready again for the full practice session

two months later, and impressed the competition with top speeds of over 190 mph down the Mulsanne straight. In the race, Phil Hill managed the fastest lap at 131 mph, but Ferrari notched up a fifth victory, continuing its stranglehold on the event with first, second and third places.

There were changes in the Ford camp following the 1964 race. There had always been a tug of war over control of the project between Ford headquarters at Dearborn, Michigan and FAV at Slough. Much of the development work in preparation for the following year was carried out in America. However, the cars continued to be built at Slough, where the team was run by John Wyer who had been Aston Martin's racing manager in their heyday.

The line-up for the 1965 Le Mans showed the seriousness with which both sides viewed their rivalry. There were 11 V-12 Ferraris and 11 Ford GT40s. The Fords were faster than the Ferraris and set a furious pace from the start. But they did not have the stamina and, by midnight, all had retired suffering from a variety of mechanical ailments. Ferrari took a record sixth Le Mans in a row.

For 1966, Ford left nothing to chance; there were 13 cars at the start: eight Mk.II prototypes with 7-litre engines, and five 4.7-litre GT versions which had been homologated for the new Sport-50 class in which at least 50 cars had to be produced for sale. This time, Ford's huge investment paid off with first, second and third places; the winning car was a 7-litre Mk. II, driven by Bruce McLaren and Chris Amon.

Ford had done it. For the next two years, the Americans reigned supreme at Le Mans until the inevitable challenge came again, this time not from Ferrari but from Porsche. The German firm had been coming to Le Mans since 1951, winning their class and steadily creeping up the overall results table, but never managing an outright victory. In 1969, it had the Sports Car World Championship in its pocket before Le Mans, with victories in the Targa Florio, at Monza, Brands Hatch and the Nürburgring. But the big prize was Le Mans and, like Ford before it, Porsche was determined to take the ultimate prize in sports-car racing.

ABOVE Watershed year at Le Mans: the start of the battle for the top title in sports-car racing between Gulf Ford and Porsche in 1969. Ford won that year, but only just.

LEFT Porsche 917 winning at Le Mans 1971. The car was driven by Gijs van Lennep and Helmut Marko.

RIGHT ABOVE Daytona is host to some of the top sports-car races in America such as the 24-hour endurance race which has been run since 1966. The Porsche 962 came second in 1985, driven by Al Holbert, Derek Bell and Al Unser Jr.

Two types of Porsche were entered: four of the older, tried and tested, 908s and two of the new and very fast 917s. Rolf Stommelen and Vic Elford, driving the 917s, went into first and second place from the start. The 917 was a brutishly powerful car. Sad proof of this came early in the race when a third 917, owned and driven by a British private entrant John Woolfe, crashed on the first lap killing him.

Porsche dominated the race but, early on the Sunday morning, Stommelen retired with a broken gearbox. Elford took over the lead in the other 917; a 908 driven by Gerard Larrousse was second and another, driven by Udo Schutz, third. The nearest

GT40, driven by Jacky Ickx, was eight laps behind the leader in fourth place. Just before 5 am, Schutz crashed, then Elford's 917 had to retire just three hours from the end with engine problems. Then another 908, which had moved up into second place, suffered the same fate, leaving Ickx in the lead. Behind him was Hans Herrmann, who had taken over the 908 from Larrousse after it had lost half an hour having a suspension fault fixed. Herrmann was closing steadily on Ickx and eventually caught up. The crowd was treated to an exciting last few laps, with the lead swapping back and forth between the two, before final victory went to Ickx in the GT40 by a few cars' lengths. Ford had its fourth victory.

But Porsche was not to be denied its place in Le Mans history. In 1970, the company was back with the 917 and Herrmann, partnered by Richard Attwood, scored its first outright win. Porsche was to dominate Le Mans more than any other name. It won again in 1971, and victory in 1976, 1977 and 1979 was followed by a run of seven successive

wins starting in 1981. With these and many more victories, Porsche established itself at the top of the league of sports-car manufacturers, its cars becoming a byword for excellence in the international sports-car marketplace.

OVERLEAF Racing for all: there are a great many people who have the urge to drive competitively and measure their driving skill under racing conditions. In Europe a business has grown up giving people their first taste of driving in a race in rally karts. The races are organized mainly for fun and for corporate entertainment and drivers need not have a racing licence or previous experience: all they need is the desire to get a sense of the thrill of racing from the driver's seat.

PAGES 194-5 Pike's Peak in Colorado is 14,110 ft high. In the nineteenth century, a carriage road was built to the summit for people to admire the view. In 1916, the road was improved to take motor vehicles and was immediately seized upon by drivers who wanted to pit their cars against its stark geography. In 1916, the Penrose Trophy for the fastest ascent up the 12-mile climb went to Rea Lantz in his home-made Romano Demon, powered by a Curtis aircraft engine; his time was 20 minutes and 55.6 seconds. In 1968, Bobby Unser was the first to do it in under 12 minutes, at 11 minutes and 54.9 seconds. In 1989, Ari Vatanen driving a Peugeot 405 Turbo 16 set the current record at 10 minutes and 48.34 seconds.

CHAPTER SEVEN

THE TEAMS

After nearly a century of competition and spectacle, motor racing at the top international level is both healthy and wealthy. It remains what it has always been: a high-technology, high-cost business. The real cost of building new cars every few years continues to creep up, but money always seems to be available to finance the technical breakthroughs and the back-up which are needed to win. Engine power has reached formidable levels. Using that power effectively to create a winning racing car has meant more investment in tyres, brakes, gearboxes, suspension, bodywork, the shape of the car itself, all of which adds to the cost. Increased costs are not confined to the car: drivers are no longer simply well-paid professionals rewarded for their driving skill. They are international superstars and are paid accordingly. And behind the scenes, a team capable of moving cars and drivers from circuit to circuit round the world has to be financed.

Fuel companies, tyre companies and some car manufacturers are very much part of motor racing, as are the spectators who go to the track. But the paymasters now include corporate sponsors, particularly those whose products are part of the good life: fashionable clothes and drinks, branded cigarettes and Swiss watches.

The last 20 years has seen the Formula One team take its position at centre stage, a coming together of drivers, designers and entrepreneurs into a tightly controlled business largely financed

LEFT Johnny Herbert making his Formula One debut with Benetton in the 1989 Brazilian Grand Prix in a Benetton B186 in which he came fourth. Benetton won its first Grand Prix in 1986, the year the Italian fashion house took over the British Toleman team as part of its world-wide promotional effort.

Some things stay the same: the power and speed of modern Formula One cars have made the Monte Carlo street circuit obsolete, but the prestige of the venue and of the race itself, which has been held on virtually the same circuit since 1929, continues to lure the World Championship circus back each year. Graham Hill, shown driving a BRM in 1964 (ABOVE), was a master of the circuit and won the race in 1963, 1964, 1965, 1968 and 1969. Nigel Mansell (Ferrari) and Derek Warwick (Lotus), fight it out for fifth and sixth place (RIGHT) along the harbour in the 1990 event, which was won by Ayrton Senna.

by a corporate giant. In 1985, the Italian fashion house Benetton sponsored the small British team Toleman; in 1986, it took the team over completely. Today it is one of the leading teams and the cars are called Benettons – high-tech, high-profile billboards for high street fashion.

Advertising on racing cars was commonplace in America, but the sport's governing bodies in Europe resisted it for many years. The turning-point came in the 1960s, a period when change was in the air and the old order was being forced to give way to a new, younger, brasher world. Advertising was finally permitted from 1 January 1968 and Colin Chapman of Lotus was one of the first to make use of the new rules to raise sponsorship. His

main source of finance was Esso, but when it pulled out in 1967 he turned to the tobacco giant John Player, who came up with the money. In exchange, the cars were in the red and gold livery of the Gold Leaf brand and Team Lotus was changed to Gold Leaf Team Lotus.

Some things have to change: the circuit of closed public roads near Reims, which had been a favourite site for the French Grand Prix, closed after Jack Brabham's triumph as driver and constructor in 1966. Reims was fast and popular, but it was a non-permanent site, one of the last in Europe to be used for World Championship races, and organizing events there was a mammoth task. The derelict pits still stand close to the public road, a forlorn monument to a bygone age.

After Charles and John Cooper, and Chapman, one of the next men to build his own cars and run his own team was Jack Brabham; the difference was he also drove for the team. Having been World Champion in 1959 and 1960, he set up a company, Motor Racing Developments, in 1961 in partnership with a fellow Australian, Ron Tauranac. They started in much the same way as the Coopers, by building racing cars to sell to private customers who wanted to race in the lower formulas. But Brabham's sights were set on Formula One and, in 1962, his first Grand Prix car, the BT3, powered by a Coventry Climax engine, made its debut at the Nürburgring with Brabham at the wheel. Later the same year, he came fourth in the United States Grand Prix at Watkins Glen, the first driver/constructor to win points in the World Drivers' Championship.

In 1964, Dan Gurney was his number two driver and gave the team its first Grand Prix victory: the French event at Rouen. In 1965, Brabham took on the New Zealand driver, Denny Hulme. In 1966, he switched to the Repco 620 engine, a racing version of a V-8 Oldsmobile, prepared by Repco,

ABOVE Jack Brabham on his way to victory in his Repco-Brabham BT20 at Zandvoort in the Dutch Grand Prix of 1966, the year he won his third World Drivers' Championship and his first Constructors' Championship.

RIGHT Bruce McLaren driving his own M7A in the British Grand Prix at Brands Hatch in 1968, in which he came seventh. The previous month he had won the Belgian Grand Prix at Spa-Francorchamps, joining Brabham as a driver/constructor winning points in the Championships.

an Australian motor parts company with interests in racing. In recognition of their support, Brabham cars became known as Repco-Brabhams.

In 1966, the formula was changed to 3 litres or 1.5 litres supercharged, but nobody went for the supercharged option. It was the 60th anniversary of the first-ever Grand Prix of 1906 at Le Mans and the French Grand Prix was quite an occasion. John Surtees was driving a Cooper with a V-12 Maserati engine as was Jochen Rindt; Brabham drove his Repco-Brabham with Hulme in another; Lotus had a mixture of Climax and BRM engines. There were two Ferraris on the front of the grid, driven by Lorenzo Bandini and Mike Parkes.

It was the last race to be held on the fast road circuit at Reims, where the fastest cars reached

ABOVE **Class of 1964: drivers before the British Grand Prix**
Back row
Tony Maggs (South Africa): 25 Grand Prix drives; Grand Prix driver 1961–5.
Jim Clark (Great Britain): World Champion 1963 and 1965; 72 Grand Prix drives, 25 victories, won Indianopolis 500 1965; killed Formula Two racing 1968.
Giancarlo Baghetti (Italy): 24 Grand Prix drives, 1 victory.
Joakim Bonnier (Sweden): 102 Grand Prix drives, 1 victory; killed racing at Le Mans 1972.
Dan Gurney (United States): 86 Grand Prix drives, 4 victories; formed all-American Formula One team (Eagle); retired 1970.
Phil Hill (United States): World Champion 1961; 48 Grand Prix drives, 3 victories; retired from Grand Prix driving 1967.
Jack Brabham (Australia): World Champion Driver 1959, 1960, 1966; World Champion Constructor 1966/1967; 126 Grand Prix drives, 14 victories; formed own team; retired from GP driving 1970; knighted 1979.
Jo Siffert (Switzerland): 97 Grand Prix drives, 2 victories; killed at Brands Hatch 1971.
Lorenzo Bandini (Italy) (half hidden): 42 Grand Prix drives, 1 victory; died after crash at Monaco 1967.
Mike Spence (Great Britain): Lotus driver 1963–6; killed in Lotus 56 turbine car at Indianapolis 500 1968.

Bruce McLaren (New Zealand): 101 Grand Prix drives, 4 victories; formed own team; killed testing sports car 1970.
Peter Revson (United States): 30 Grand Prix drives, 2 victories; killed testing car 1974.
Chris Amon (New Zealand): 96 Grand Prix drives, no victories; youngest driver in Grand Prix at 19; formed own team which was unsuccessful; retired 1976.
Graham Hill (Great Britain): World Champion 1962, 1968; 176 Grand Prix drives, 14 victories; won Indianapolis 500 1966; longest-ever career in World Championship racing (16 years); started own team 1973; killed in aircraft crash 1975.
Front row
Richie Ginther (United States): 52 Grand Prix drives, 1 victory; died 1989.
Bob Anderson (Rhodesia): ex-racing motor cyclist; killed testing at Silverstone 1967.
John Taylor (Great Britain): raced 1964–6; killed in German Grand Prix 1966.
Mike Hailwood (Great Britain): World Motor Cycle Champion 10 times: European Formula Two Champion 1972; 50 Grand Prix drives, no victories; killed in road accident 1981.

RIGHT ABOVE **Jackie Stewart** (Great Britain): World Champion 1969, 1971, 1973; 99 Grand Prix drives, 27 victories; retired 1973.

around 180 mph in practice down the long straight past the pits. Bandini and Brabham battled for the lead from the start, both drivers breaking the lap record during the early stages of the race. Bandini managed to pull steadily away from Brabham, who was well ahead of the second Ferrari. Parkes was in third place. Halfway through the race, only the Brabhams and the Ferraris were in contention, with Bandini continuing to open his lead over Brabham. Then the Ferrari's throttle linkage broke and Brabham was suddenly in the lead. He did enough to hold Parkes at bay to win by 9.5 seconds; Hulme was third. It was the first Grand Prix victory for a driver/contructor. It was Brabham's year: he won the British, Dutch and German Grands Prix to take a third World Drivers' title for himself and, the first driver to do so in a car of his own manufacture, the Constructors' title for the Brabham team.

Brabham was not alone in turning driver/constructor during the 1960s. The New Zealand driver Bruce McLaren had made his name as the youngest driver ever to win a Grand Prix when, at the age of 22, he came first in the American event in 1959. In 1966, his company started building cars around BRM engines and, within two years, he had notched up his first World Championship points in his own car.

Ken Tyrrell, who had started as a driver in 500 cc Cooper-Nortons and had later managed the BMC-Cooper team, established the Tyrrell Racing Organization in 1963, concentrating on the lower formulas. He had a great eye for good drivers and signed up a young Scot called Jackie Stewart, initially for Formula Three. Frank Williams, himself a Formula Three driver, established Frank Williams (Racing Cars) Ltd in 1968, racing Brabham Formula Two cars.

They were the new breed of entrepreneurs, men who had worked in the motor-racing business and loved it, who formed partnerships and put together the money and the expertise to create small, flexible teams. They became known as the 'kit-car' builders because, unlike the more established names such as Ferrari and BRM and, before them, Alfa Romeo and Maserati, they put their cars together from components which they bought separately. Enzo

ABOVE LEFT Nigel Mansell: Britain's top driver in 1991. Until 1991, the closest he came to winning the World Drivers' title was in 1986 when he needed to be third or better in the Australian Grand Prix to clinch the Championship. He was lying third when a tyre burst, putting him out of the race and giving Frenchman Alain Prost the title.

ABOVE RIGHT Ayrton Senna (Brazil): first Grand Prix for Toleman 1984, drove for Lotus 1985-7, then moved to McLaren; World Champion 1988, 1990.

Ferrari, ever slow to see when change was at hand, dismissed them as mere '*assemblatore*' – but these young men were about to transform the sport.

With the formula change of 1966, Coventry Climax stopped building racing engines and left the kit-car builders without an engine. Its decision also left a hole in the market. Chapman, as dynamic and far-sighted as ever, went to Ford, with whom he had a good working relationship based on his success at the Indianapolis 500 the previous year, and suggested they fund the development of a Formula One engine. Ford agreed and backed Cosworth Engineering, a small Northampton company owned by Keith Duckworth and Mike Costin, who had developed an existing Ford engine, the 116E from the Cortina saloon car, for Formula Two. They had already produced a Type A, 4-cylinder engine called the FVA (for Four Valve A) and because the new engine would be twice that, a V-8, it became known as the DFV (for Double Four Valve). It was a perfect piece of design: a compact, light, 3-litre engine with double overhead camshafts and four valves per cylinder and fuel injection. It took five months to build the first one and, when it was tested, it produced slightly over the target output of 400 bhp.

The engine was ready to be installed in a car in April. Chapman had specified the lightest and simplest chassis to take the new engine, and that is what the Lotus team of engineers and designers, led by Maurice Phillippe, produced. After some tests the new car, the Lotus-Cosworth 49, made its debut on 4 June 1967 at the Dutch Grand Prix at Zandvoort. Chapman had two of the finest drivers at the time: the incomparable Jim Clark and the tireless Graham Hill.

Hill managed the fastest practice lap in one of the new cars, then led from the start of the race. A battle developed behind him for second place, involving most of the stars of the day: Brabham, the reigning World Champion, Chris Amon for Ferrari, Rindt in a Cooper-Maserati and Gurney driving an American-backed Eagle-Weslake. After eight laps, Hill's new car came into the pits with a camshaft drive broken, but by lap 16 Clark had managed to fight his way through the field into the lead. He steadily widened the gap to win from Brabham by 24 seconds – the Lotus 49 had won its maiden race.

The Lotus drivers notched up nine pole positions in 1967, and Clark won the British, United States and Mexican Grands Prix. At the Italian event he was in pole position alongside Brabham and McLaren. Amon, driving for Ferrari, was the favourite with the crowd. Surtees was driving a Honda and Gurney an Eagle-Weslake. It was an exciting start with Brabham, Gurney and McLaren hurtling away early in a cloud of smoke while Amon nearly rammed Clark from behind. By lap three, Clark was in the lead. By lap five, Hill was behind him with Hulme, Brabham's number two, in third position when Clark had a puncture and had to go into the pits. The leading cars completed a full lap before he rejoined behind them, but within five laps he had passed them, pulling his team-mate Hill into the lead with his slipstream as he went by, before forging ahead with a lap to make up.

Then Hill's engine gave up and Brabham took over the lead as Clark gained ground. It was a legendary performance. He overtook the leading pair, Brabham and Surtees, then suddenly, on the last lap, started slowing down because of a fuel-feed problem. They passed him again. Surtees and Brabham contested the race right to the line, Surtees winning for Honda by a whisker. After driving one of the best races of his career, Clark came third.

It was a great debut year for the Lotus 49 and the Cosworth engine. Clark came third in the Driver's Championship, which went to Hulme; Brabham, his boss, was second.

For 1967, Chapman had had exclusive use of the DFV engine, but from 1968 it was available to all the teams at a price of around £7500. McLaren bought DFVs and so did Ken Tyrrell, even though he had no chassis to put them in. He approached Matra, the French aerospace company which fielded its own racing team using Matra V-12 engines. Tyrrell raced in 1968 as Matra International; effectively, Matra had two teams, one powered by its own 400-bhp engine and one by the 410-bhp Ford-Cosworth DFVs.

Lotus had had the advantage of a year to settle down with the new engine, and was clear favourite for the Championships in 1968. Clark won the first event of the season, the South African Grand Prix at Kyalami, bringing his total of Grand Prix victories to 25. But it was his last triumph: he was killed in a Formula Two race at Hockenheim in Germany. Chapman and the team were shattered by the loss but, undaunted, Hill went on winning and took the World Championship for himself and the Constructors' title for Lotus. It was a bitter-sweet success.

Such was the power of the DFV engine that designers were faced with the problem of how to transmit that power to the road via the narrow tyres of the time. Different ways of increasing traction were developed during the following years: tyres became wider, softer and stickier and there were experiments with six-wheeled cars and with four-wheel drive. But one of the most effective ways to increase traction was to use aerodynamics to create a downforce on the car. A wing, or aerofoil, shaped just like an aircraft wing, was positioned on struts above the wheels, but was inverted so that the force was directed downwards.

In 1968, Brabham, Lotus and Ferrari all experimented with aerofoils. Brabham and Ferrari used wings mounted on the car as a whole, but Chapman went a stage further, mounting a wing on the suspension struts so that it acted more directly on the wheels. The advantage of aerofoils was increased traction, which made better use of the power from the engine and led to better roadholding, which in turn led to fast cornering; the disadvantage was that they added to drag by increasing wind resistance, especially on fast straights where they reduced speed. The next logical step was to make the aerofoil movable, changing the angle to give less downforce and less wind resistance on the straight, then reapplying the downforce in the corners where it was most useful. Lotus and Matra experimented with movable wings actuated by electric motors.

Aerodynamics: during practice for the Monaco Grand Prix in 1969, all the cars, including Bruce McLaren's M7C (BELOW), were fitted with high-mounted wings to create a downforce on the wheels, improving traction and roadholding. But they were considered dangerous and were banned for the race. Strict controls on the use of aerodynamics were subsequently introduced and led to more compact-looking devices such as those on Jackie Stewart's Tyrrell 003 (OVERLEAF) at Monaco in 1971, a race he won.

The aerofoil offered an advance in the technology of the racing car, but there were crashes and a number of people were not happy about the development. It took a brush with death to get aerodynamics under control. The Lotus drivers Hill and Rindt were both driving Lotus 49s with aerofoils in the 1969 Spanish Grand Prix, which was held on a street circuit in Barcelona. Rindt was fastest in practice, and went into the lead followed by Amon in a Ferrari. There was a left-hand bend just after the pits and, coming out of it, a dip in the road. The cars lifted up as they came out of the dip at speed, rather like going over a humpback bridge. On the ninth lap Hill, lying third, went into the bend as usual but as his car came out of the dip the rear-mounted aerofoil collapsed. Suddenly robbed of the downforce his car slid wide, smashing into the safety barrier. Hill was unhurt.

Rindt then roared past and Hill saw what he thought might be the cause of his own crash: Rindt's aerofoil was bent in the middle. The aerofoils had not been stressed to take the forces which

were applied as the car lifted up coming out of the dip: under the strain they had steadily weakened, then broken. Hill attempted to get a warning to Rindt to stop on the next lap, but he was too late. What had happened to Hill's car happened to the second Lotus in exactly the same spot: Rindt spun off as Hill had done. The Lotus hit Hill's wrecked car and overturned and Rindt was seriously injured.

Rindt had been opposed to wings and, after the race, he made his views known in an open letter. He believed not only that they could be dangerous, but also that they were in no way linked to the improvement of cars in general and therefore had no place on racing cars. By the time the Grand Prix circus had arrived in Monaco for the next race, wings were the topic on everybody's lips. They were used in the first practice session, then an emergency meeting of the Commission Sportive Internationale (CSI), the body delegated by the FIA to control the sport, banned them. The teams were furious because their cars performed better with aerofoils, but they had no option and they were all removed. Hill, who had a particular affinity with the Monaco circuit, won the race.

After the Dutch Grand Prix, the CSI permitted smaller wings which were not movable and not fitted to the unsprung parts of the car. Aerodynamics had been tamed for the moment.

The two great protagonists at the top of Formula One at this time were Tyrrell, and Chapman at Lotus. Tyrrell's first DFV-powered Matra, the MS10, made its debut at the controversial Monaco race in 1968 driven by Jackie Stewart, who had been racing in Formula Two for Tyrrell and in Formula One for BRM until Tyrrell had built a suitable car. At the Dutch Grand Prix which followed, Stewart gave Tyrrell his first Grand Prix victory, beating the Matra-powered Matra of Jean-Pierre Beltoise into second place. In 1969, Tyrrell brought out the DFV-powered MS80 for Stewart, who won six Grands Prix in the car and became World Champion. But the Matra-Tyrrell relationship had to end when Matra linked up with the French manufacturer Simca, part of the Chrysler group. Chrysler could not have one of its subsidiaries racing a Ford-engined car, so Tyrrell had to look elsewhere. He decided to build his own but, as an interim measure, bought a March 701 F1 car for Stewart for the 1970 season.

With most teams using the same engine, Chapman was always looking for a new advantage. Aerofoils had been restricted, so he turned to the overall design of the body and made it 'wedge' shaped to create a downforce, following the design of the Lotus 56, a turbine-powered car which he had developed for the Indianapolis 500.

The new Lotus 72 Formula One car was demonstrated to the Press in April 1970. It was wedge-shaped with front winglets, and a triple layer of aerofoils at the rear which were within the CSI restrictions. The radiators had been moved from the front to the side of the car, making it aerodynamically cleaner and at the same time reducing the heat in the cockpit so that it was more comfortable for the driver.

The Lotus team consisted of Rindt and John Miles. Rindt won the Dutch, British and German

Grands Prix and was leading the World Drivers' Championship table at the time of the Italian Grand Prix at Monza. During practice, he was driving a Lotus 72 without the wing attached; coming into the 'Curva Parabolica' he braked from full speed, something gave way and he ploughed into the left-hand barrier and was killed. For the first time, the World Championship was awarded posthumously.

In 1971, the advantage swung back to Tyrrell and Stewart. Tyrrell had unveiled the first car of his own design, the 001, late in the 1970 season. By the start of the following year, its teething troubles had been sorted out: Stewart won six Grands Prix and took the title.

The advantage returned to Lotus in 1972. Chapman had two new drivers, Emerson Fittapaldi from Brazil and Reine Wisell. The Lotus 72s were clad in a new livery: the all-black with a fine gold line of John Player Special cigarettes had replaced the gold and red of Gold Leaf. Fittipaldi won five Grands Prix and took the Drivers' Championship.

In 1973, Ronnie Peterson replaced Wisell at Lotus, and at Tyrrell François Cevert partnered Stewart who was on top form. Stewart passed Clark's record total of 25 Grand Prix wins, taking his total to 27 and, by the time of the United States Grand Prix, had the World Championship sewn up. Then Cevert was killed in practice for the race and Tyrrell withdrew the team. With a third World Drivers' title under his belt, Stewart retired from racing to concentrate on his business interests.

The years 1966 to 1973 were years of triumph for the British-based kit-car manufacturers, and their success continued into 1974, when Fittipaldi won the World Drivers' Championship driving for McLaren. McLaren had been killed testing a sports car in 1970 but the team survived, sponsored by Yardley cosmetics. The smaller teams were becoming a force in the sport and, realizing their strength, they formed the Formula One Constructors' Association (FOCA) to look after

OVERLEAF Tyrrell-Cosworth 006: this car was built for Jackie Stewart's final season of Grand Prix racing in 1973, the year he won his third World Drivers' Championship with four victories in the Belgian, Monaco, Dutch and German Grands Prix. It is preserved in the Donington Museum.

their interests. The guiding force behind FOCA was Bernard Ecclestone, who had bought the Brabham team in 1971 after Brabham had retired. The FOCA teams, most of them British based, wanted to maximize their rewards from the sport, and the new organization negotiated with tracks for start money and for a prize fund to be established. It even arranged cheap flights. The teams quickly found that they had considerable power when they spoke with one voice.

In 1975, the firm the '*assemblatore*' had most successfully pushed aside, the leader of the old guard of racing-car makers – Ferrari – made a comeback. During the late 1960s and early 1970s Enzo Ferrari found the cost of staying in competitive Formula One and in sports-car racing too great. After the deal with Ford had fallen through, he looked to Italian industry for financial assistance and in 1969 he sold out to the giant Fiat conglomerate. By 1975, Fiat wanted results.

In 1970, Ferrari had brought out the 312 with a 3-litre, 12-cylinder engine which gave about 460 bhp, but it had not done well against the kit-car teams in the early 1970s. In 1975, it came out as the 312T. The 'T' stood for *transversale* and referred to the gearbox which had been installed across the car to improve weight distribution. The engine had been boosted to 500 bhp. The Ferrari drivers were the Austrian Niki Lauda, and the Swiss Gianclaudio 'Clay' Regazzoni. Lauda won the Monaco, Belgian, Swedish, French and United States Grands Prix taking the Drivers' Championship; Regazzoni won the German race to give Ferrari their first Constructors' title since 1964.

Ferrari was back at the top, but in 1976 it faced a formidable challenge from the kit-car fraternity in the form of McLaren, who had taken on a new British driver, James Hunt. Lauda started the season well, and was leading the championship table, when he had a near-fatal crash at the Nürburgring during the German Grand Prix and missed the next three races. By the last race of the season, the Japanese Grand Prix, he was still in the lead in the championship with Hunt only three points behind. Depending on the placings, Hunt could take the title.

Neither Lauda nor Hunt managed to get pole position at the Fuji circuit. That went to Mario Andretti, the star American driver, who was now driving for Lotus. The day of the race was misty and rain-soaked; there were great puddles of water all over the track and when Hunt went into the lead, Lauda found himself driving in a huge cloud of spray. Lauda did two laps, decided that it was too dangerous and retired, handing Hunt the championship provided he could stay in the race and finish third. After nine laps Hunt had to come in for a tyre change and rejoined in fifth place; he was unaware of his place at the time. With the Championship in the balance, he could not afford to relax so he pushed as hard as he could, passing anybody he came across to finish third behind Patrick Depailler in a Tyrrell and the winner, Andretti. He was World Champion by a single point.

Lauda's decision was a brave one. He faced a barrage of criticism in the Italian popular press and Enzo Ferrari was not best pleased. Relations were strained during the following season, but in spite of that – and that in the end was the measure of the man – Lauda won the Drivers' Championship and the Constructors' title for Ferrari. He continued with Ferrari in 1977, then drove for Brabham in 1978, coming fourth in the World Championship. He retired from racing in 1979.

The Lotus 72 had been a highly successful car for Chapman, but, by 1977, it was old. Chapman came up with a new idea to gain an advantage: to use the underside of the car to produce a downforce, a process known as 'ground effect'. Instead of being mounted as external wings, the aerofoil shape was built into pods on either side of the car producing a low pressure area underneath, a device which sucked the car to the track. Side panels, or 'skirts', very close to the ground stopped air filling the low pressure area. Theoretically, if the downforce was greater than the weight of the car, it would stick even to an upside-down track.

The Lotus design team developed the pods using models in wind tunnels and, once they had the right shape, installed them on the Lotus 78. Much of the testing was carried out by Andretti

who had forged a close relationship with Chapman. The car was unveiled in December 1976 and Andretti won four Grands Prix the following season. There were teething problems and a string of failures kept it out of the running for the 1977 championships, but in 1978 the 78 was refined into the Lotus 79 and it put Lotus back on top: Andretti won six World Championship events to take both the Drivers' and the Constructors' titles.

LEFT Mario Andretti: US National Champion 1965, 1966, 1969, World Champion 1978; 128 Grand Prix drives, 12 victories; won Indianapolis 500 1969; one of the select group of drivers to reach the top on both sides of the Atlantic. In 1978, he drove John Player Special Lotus 78s and 79s to victory in six Grands Prix, including the Dutch event (BELOW) at Zandvoort; team-mate Ronnie Peterson came second.

Closeness to danger remains one of the attractions of motor racing. Shortly after the start of the 1975 Indianapolis 500, Tom Sneva touched the wheel of another car and slammed into the safety barrier at 150 mph, sending spectators scattering. The methanol fuel caught fire as the car disintegrated in front of the grandstands; Sneva was lucky to escape with minor injuries.

OVERLEAF When Tom Sneva crashed again in 1985, the safety crew was quickly on the spot and his car was doused with fire-suppressant material.

RENAULT'S RENAISSANCE

The French car manufacturer Renault has won the French Grand Prix twice in the event's history – once in 1906 and once in 1979. On both occasions the company was innovative: in 1906, it used detachable wheel rims and in 1979 it used turbocharged engines. Renault stopped racing in 1908. The company returned 60 years later, in the early 1970s, to rallying, sports-car racing and Formula Two events. Renault started work in 1972 on a 2-litre V6 turbocharged engine, designed to beat Porsche at Le Mans. At the same time, it developed a 1.5-litre version to comply with the long-dormant supercharged class in Formula One.

The turbocharged Renault RS01 made its debut at the British Grand Prix in 1977, driven by Jean-Pierre Jabouille. It produced 500 bhp at 11000 rpm, but Jabouille started 21st on the grid and retired early; nobody took turbocharging as a serious threat to the 'atmospherically aspirated' cars (i.e. cars which had no system for forcing fuel into the engine). In 1978, Renault won the Le Mans 24-hour race, then concentrated all its efforts on Formula One. Jabouille gained the first pole position for a turbocharged car in the South African Grand Prix in 1979, and won the French event the same year.

But Renault never really benefited from its pioneering work with turbochargers. It was a huge, nationalized company and its racing department was no match for the highly competitive, single-minded men behind the kit-car teams. By the mid-1980s, all teams were using turbochargers and, in 1985, with little to show for their investment, Renault pulled out of racing. It continues to supply engines to teams such as Lotus and Williams.

RIGHT Jean-Pierre Jabouille drove in 49 Grands Prix and won two; he was badly injured in a crash at the Canadian Grand Prix in 1980, and retired from Grand Prix racing the following year.

BELOW First turbocharged car on pole position: Jabouille in the RS10 in the 1979 South African Grand Prix. He was unplaced.

FAR RIGHT AND BELOW RIGHT First turbocharged car to win: Jabouille at the French Grand Prix at Dijon in 1979. René Arnoux was third in another Renault.

Like all the kit-car teams, Lotus still used the Cosworth DFV engine which had dominated Formula One racing throughout the 1970s. It was one of the pillars on which it had built its success, but during the late 1970s a challenge to that supremacy had begun to develop. Renault, one of the greatest names from the distant past of Grand Prix racing, decided to compete again. Instead of following the other teams with their 3-litre engines, Renault decided to go for the 1.5-litre option using turbochargers. Unlike the mechanically driven supercharger, the turbocharger uses a small turbine driven by the exhaust gases to drive the compressor which forces fuel into the engine.

Renault entered its first turbocharged car, the RS01, in five Grands Prix in 1977 but it failed to finish any of them. It persevered, putting enormous amounts of money into the project, and gained its first Championship points with Jean-Pierre Jabouille at the wheel in 1978. In 1979, it looked as if Renault's investment might be beginning to pay off when Jabouille won the French Grand Prix at Dijon in the Renault RS10 in front of an ecstatic French crowd.

In the following season, Renault brought out the RE20; the RE stood for Renault Elf, after the French oil company that sponsored the team. The 'turbo' engine was producing 520 bhp and Renault was favourite for the 1980 Championships. It had two French drivers, Jabouille who won one Grand Prix and René Arnoux who won two, but a series of minor failures cost Renault valuable points. The Cosworth engines were less powerful than the Renault ones, but most of the teams were using ground-effect cars modelled on the Lotus 79 to hold off the turbocharged challenge. Although the kit-car makers could not afford the investment needed for turbocharging, they remained on top with the Australian driver, Alan Jones, taking the World Drivers' and Constructors' titles for Williams in the FW07.

A technical divide was opening up between the kit-car teams who had invested in ground-effect cars, and names like Ferrari, Alfa Romeo, who was making a comeback, and Renault. With their greater resources, the big firms were all pursuing turbocharging. These technical divisions coincided with another split in the ranks of the competitors, this time a political one. It had been developing for some time and now came to a head. The issue was control of Formula One racing and the protagonists were the governing body, the Fédération Internationale du Sport Automobile (FISA) which had superseded the CSI in 1978 and was represented by its president Jean-Marie Balestre, and FOCA, represented by Ecclestone. Thanks mainly to the efforts of FOCA, Formula One and the World Championships had become a lucrative business with a high international profile. FOCA had represented the kit-car teams well and, from its position of strength based on a united front, had negotiated better prize and starting money, and better financial deals with track owners and, in particular, with television broadcasters. FISA felt that it was losing its grip on the sport. The political division was on the same lines as the technical split: Ferrari, Renault and Alfa Romeo sided with FISA and most of the kit-car makers sided with FOCA. The technical and political issues inevitably became intertwined.

In 1979, FISA decreed that the skirts which helped to create the ground effect would be banned in the 1981 season. The smaller teams saw this as favouring the larger companies with their turbocharger technology by taking away the advantage which ground effects gave them. FISA also introduced mandatory briefings for drivers before races and fined some drivers who did not attend them. By the time of the 1980 Spanish Grand Prix, the drivers still had not paid the fines and FISA decreed that they could not race until they did. FOCA responded by saying that its teams would not take part unless the fines were withdrawn. FISA stood firm, but the Spanish organizers altered the sanctioning arrangements, making it effectively a non-FISA race. Ferrari, Alfa Romeo and Renault pulled out; the FOCA teams raced. Alan Jones won for Williams, but the points did not count towards the World Championships. Battle had been joined and a split between FOCA and FISA looked like a possibility; at one stage it appeared that two parallel championships were going to be run.

ABOVE **Mansell and Piquet** took first and second place in the 1986 British Grand Prix. They repeated the double in 1987, much to the delight of the British fans.

RIGHT ABOVE **Mansell on his** way to victory in the San Marino Grand Prix in 1987.

FAR RIGHT ABOVE **Frank** Williams in the pits at the Austrian Grand Prix in 1987 watching Mansell win again for the team. In 1986, at the height of the team's success, Williams had been paralysed from the waist down after a road accident, but his will to win was undiminished.

RIGHT **The line-up at the** Williams factory at Didcot, Oxfordshire.

WILLIAMS

Frank Williams is one of the thrusting, entrepreneurial team-owners, with a will to win, who have reached the top of the sport and transformed it in the process. His team, Williams Grand Prix Engineering, became a force to be reckoned with in Formula One in 1979 when it introduced its Cosworth-engined FW07. Its first Grand Prix victory came in 1979 when Clay Regazzoni won the British event; in 1980, Alan Jones took the Drivers' Championship for Williams, who also took the Constructors' title. Another Constructors' title followed in 1981 and Keke Rosberg took the Drivers' title in 1982 with the improved FW08. Williams changed to turbo-charged engines in 1983 in an exclusive deal with the Japanese firm, Honda. By 1985, the team, was back on top with the FW10 and in 1986 it took the Constructors' Cup with Nelson Piquet and Nigel Mansell. Mansell narrowly missed the Drivers' title and Piquet took it in 1987. For the 1988 season, Honda switched its allegiance to McLaren and Lotus and Williams turned first to Judd engines and then to Renault, but the team was eclipsed by the Honda-engined McLarens in the late 1980s. Mansell moved to Ferrari, but returned to Williams for 1991.

The manoeuvring hotted up in 1981, when FISA insisted on its rules about skirts being applied in World Championship events. Neither side would compromise and the first race of the season, the Argentinian Grand Prix, was cancelled. The World Championships had reached a low point and cancelling races did neither side any good. So the teams held a meeting in Maranello, Enzo Ferrari's home town, and the grand old man of motor racing helped to formulate an agreement. Before it could be put into effect, the South African Grand Prix was held on 7 February as a FOCA-only event with the previous year's rules applying on skirts. Consequently, the points which Carlos Reutemann would have gained by winning for Williams did not count towards either the Drivers' or the Constructors' Championship.

The Concorde Agreement, which settled the dispute between FISA and FOCA, was finally reached in March and a programme of races agreed for the rest of the 1981 season. The teams acknowledged FISA's position as regulator of the sport, but FOCA retained its right to negotiate with organizers and television companies, though in co-operation with FISA. There was a compromise over the rules on skirts, which had to have a clearance of 6 cm when the car was standing in the pit lane.

The smaller teams had reached their prominent position by their engineering ingenuity and flexibility, and it did not take them long to find a way round the new skirt rules. Gordon Murray of Brabham developed a suspension system which enabled the drivers to lower the cars on the track, then raise them in the pits for checking. Chapman came up with an even more ingenious idea: he built the Lotus 88 which had two chassis, one of which was sucked to the ground to produce the ground effect. However, there were protests all round when it made its first appearance and it was banned.

In the championships, Williams took the Constructors' title. The Drivers' title went to the Brazilian, Nelson Piquet for Brabham by one point from Reutemann, driving for Williams. Had the South African result counted, Reutemann would have been champion.

Despite the Concorde Agreement, the sniping between the two sides continued during 1982. The minimum weight limit was set at a point which favoured the heavier turbo-powered cars; the smaller cars had to carry ballast to bring them up to the weight. Both Brabham and Williams fitted water tanks, ostensibly to provide a cooling system for the brakes but in fact the water was released during the race to make the cars lighter; the tanks were topped up afterwards to pass the scrutineers. In the Brazilian Grand Prix, Piquet, driving for Brabham, and Keke Rosberg, driving for Williams, used the device and came first and second only to be disqualified later. The race was left to the third-placed Renault driven by Alain Prost. The FOCA teams responded by boycotting the San Marino Grand Prix but, despite this, Rosberg won the Drivers' title in a Williams. The Constructors' title went to Ferrari.

In 1983, the dispute subsided. Ground effects were banned; all cars had to have flat undersides. By then, the smaller teams were coming to terms with turbocharged engines. Chapman had arranged to use Renault engines the previous year, but died of a heart attack before they were used. Williams made a deal with Honda to develop an engine but it was not ready for the early part of the season. Brabham had made arrangements with BMW in 1981. After all the investment by the big teams, it was ironic that the first turbocharged victory in the Drivers' Championship went to a driver from one of the smaller teams: Piquet, driving a Brabham-BMW.

Renault was not well-rewarded for its pioneering work on turbos. By 1985, its EF15 engine produced over 800 bhp and other teams were buying it. But its team, as part of a big company, could not match the competitive ethos of the smaller ones and after a decade of expensive effort Renault withdrew from racing, though it continued to supply engines to other teams. Alfa Romeo had developed its own turbocharged engine, but it was not competitive and the company also pulled out in 1985. Of the grand old names, only Ferrari remained, taking the World Constructors' Championship in 1982 and 1983.

The early 1980s had been dominated by Brabham and Williams, but from 1984 McLaren took over. The team had been at the top since Hunt's win in 1976. In 1980, after active pressure from its sponsors Philip Morris, manufacturers of Marlboro cigarettes, it merged with Project 4, a successful Formula Two team run by Ron Dennis, who had started racing as a mechanic in the Cooper team in the days of Jack Brabham. With him came John Barnard, a British designer who had been working in America. Dennis and Barnard became the major figures at McLaren with a completely new car, the MP4.

The new McLaren embodied another technical advance: the first use of carbon fibre to make monocoque. It came out in 1981, still using a Cosworth engine, and John Watson drove it to its first Grand Prix victory at the British event that year. It was the first win for a car with a carbon-fibre monocoque, and McLaren's first victory since 1977. For once, Chapman came second with a technical innovation.

Enter carbon-fibre: John Barnard (ABOVE). The man behind the MP4, he pioneered the use of carbon-fibre monocoques in Formula One, then moved to Ferrari in 1986 and Benetton in 1990. John Watson in the McLaren-Ford MP4 on his way to sixth place in the 1981 Austrian event (BELOW); a month previously, he had won the British Grand Prix in the car, the first time a Grand Prix had been won by a car with a carbon-fibre monocoque.

In the same year, McLaren brought Niki Lauda out of retirement and Watson and Lauda won two Grands Prix each, putting the team in second place behind Ferrari in the Constructors' title. Watson came second in the Drivers' Championship – McLaren was on the march.

By 1983, Barnard was arranging for a turbocharged engine for the MP4. He wanted one tailor-made to his specification, not off the peg, and he wanted exclusivity. He went to Porsche, who agreed to build what he wanted with financial backing from a French firm, Techniques d'Avant Garde (TAG), and the engine was ready by the end of the 1983 season.

In 1984, Alain Prost joined Lauda at McLaren. They were unstoppable: Prost won six Grands Prix and Lauda took five, giving him his third World Champion title by half a point from his team-mate and McLaren-TAG its first Constructors' Championship. Prost continued the winning streak, taking the Drivers' title for the next two years.

Williams broke McLaren's run in 1987. Its victory was the result of a partnership with Honda, whose engine proved to be a race winner. The drivers were Piquet and the British driver, Nigel Mansell. Mansell won six Grands Prix, Piquet won three, but Piquet managed a more consistent season overall to win the Drivers' title. Between them, Mansell and Piquet gave Williams the Constructors' title by 135 points to McLaren's 76. In 1988, Honda switched to McLaren who signed the brilliant young Brazilian driver, Ayrton Senna.

The combination of car, engine, drivers and team worked like a dream: between them, Senna and Prost won 15 out of the 16 World Championship events in 1988, an unprecedented record. They were in the same team, but they were the greatest of personal rivals. Often out in front together, in identical cars, they provided the World Championships with the competitiveness and spectacle which makes motor racing such a popular sport. The Drivers' title was in the balance between them until the last Grand Prix in Japan. Senna

LEFT **Nigel Mansell's Williams-Honda FW10, in which he won his first Grand Prix at Brands Hatch in 1985.**

DAYTONA SUPERSPEEDWAY

Today, stock-car racing is the most popular form of
motor sport in the USA; the Daytona 500 race is the jewel
in the crown of NASCAR racing. The cars (RIGHT) have very
little connection with the production cars which their shapes
represent: they reach well over 200 mph, their chassis are
strengthened and the bodywork, which is very similar to their
production counterparts, is built around a strong cage made of
tubular steel. The 1988 race (ABOVE) was won by Bobby Allison
in a Miller-Buick.

stalled at the start, but went on to win from Prost.
He took the World Drivers' Championship by three
points, winning a record of eight Grands Prix in
the process and beating Clark's record of seven –
which Prost had equalled in 1984. Between them,
Senna and Prost amassed 199 points in the Constructors' title – more than the next eight teams put
together.

LEFT Ron Dennis: the ultimate team boss in the 1980s, Dennis is the man behind the emergence of McLaren as Formula One's top team. The team is on a sound financial footing under a sponsorship deal with Marlboro cigarettes, one of the biggest sponsors in motor racing. Today, the names associated with the kit-car era are high-technology businesses that manufacture all the parts of their cars, except the engines, themselves.

BELOW Ayrton Senna and the Honda team at the 1989 Italian Grand Prix. Honda was the power behind McLaren and Senna's spectacular success in 1988. Turbochargers were banned from 1989 and engine size was limited to 3.5 litres, all engines breathing air through carburettors.

RIGHT Prost, having moved to Ferrari in 1990, winning the Brazilian Grand Prix that year against his rival Senna, a Brazilian on his home ground. But Senna took the Drivers' Championship.

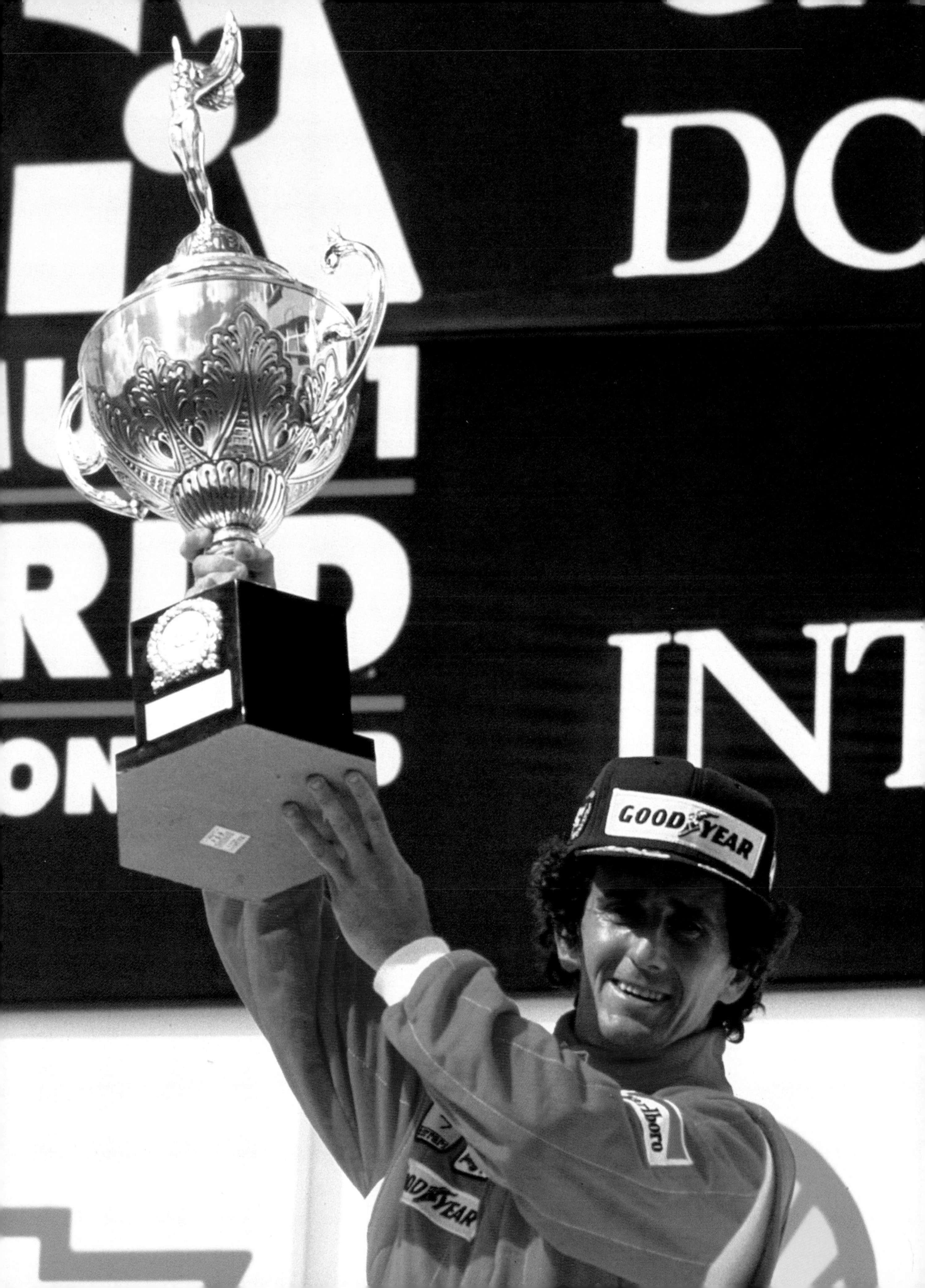
GOOD YEAR

In 1989, the closing races of the season were a showdown between the pair. Prost was leading the Drivers' Championship table, and Senna would have to win the last three Grands Prix to stay in the running. Victory in any of them would give Prost the title. Tension between the two was high and it was widely reported that they had not exchanged so much as a word for months. Senna won in Spain, then the circus moved on to Suzuka for the Japanese Grand Prix. Prost went into the lead with Senna hard on his heels. Coming into a corner, Senna tried to overtake but Prost held his line, not giving way. The two McLarens came together, touched and slid off the track side by side. Prost got out of his car, but Senna was push-started by the marshals, drove across the corner and rejoined the race. He made a pit stop for a new nose to be fitted, then tore off after Alessandro Nannini, who had taken the lead for Benetton, and overtook him to win just before the finish.

Senna was disqualified for missing out part of the circuit when he drove across the corner to rejoin the race, and Nannini was declared the winner. As a result, Prost was World Champion for the third time in his career. His rival was later given a six-month suspended ban and was fined $100,000 by FISA. In 1990, the super-competitive Senna won the title back.

Today, the specialized team has become the backbone of Formula One and the World Championships. It has taken over what the pioneer car builders started. What began as an adjunct of the motor industry, has become a big, and quite distinct, business. It remains part of the motor industry, but it is also part of the entertainment and advertising industries.

It is a truly twentieth-century spectacle: a festival of speed and technical excellence, a triumph of commercialism, a piece of popular culture, but above all a contest between individuals.

The longest track record in the World Championships: Ferraris have raced in every year of the Championship since it was started in 1950. When Enzo Ferrari died in 1988, aged 90, his cars had competed in over 400 World Championship races. The team continues to compete at the top of Formula One. Alain Prost (LEFT) on Ferrari's home territory at the San Marino Grand Prix in 1990.

The lifeblood of motor racing is the enthusiasm of its spectators, and Ferrari has particularly enthusiastic fans known as 'Tifosi'. Here they are cheering Prost during practice for the 1990 San Marino Grand Prix. Never mind that the driver is French – the crowd's loyalty is to the red cars which race for Italy.

Record prize: in 1991 Rick Mears, driving for the Penske team, became the third man in history to win the US classic race, the Indianapolis 500, four times. The team's purse was $1,219,704.

INDEX